The MAP of HEAVEN

*A neurosurgeon explores the mysteries
of the afterlife and the truth
about what lies beyond*

DR EBEN ALEXANDER
with Ptolemy Tompkins

piatkus

PIATKUS

First published in the US in 2014 Simon & Schuster, US
First published in Great Britain in 2014 by Piatkus

A CIP catalogue record for this book
is available from the British Library.

ISBN 978-0-349-40351-9

Printed and bound in Great Britain by
Clays Ltd, St Ives plc

Papers used by Piatkus are from well-managed forests
and other responsible sources.

MIX
Paper from
responsible sources
FSC® C104740

Piatkus
An imprint of
Little, Brown Book Group
100 Victoria Embankment
London EC4Y 0DY

An Hachette UK Company
www.hachette.co.uk

www.piatkus.co.uk

*To all courageous souls whose loving hearts yearn
toward the truth of our existence.*

Contents

Introduction

I am the child of earth and starry heaven, but my real race is of heaven.
—FRAGMENT FROM AN ANCIENT GREEK TEXT
GIVING INSTRUCTIONS FOR THE NEWLY DEAD SOUL
ON HOW TO NAVIGATE THE AFTERLIFE

Imagine a young couple at their wedding. The ceremony is over, and everyone is crowding around on the church steps for a photo. But the couple, at this particular moment, doesn't notice them. They're too concerned with each other. They are looking deep into each other's eyes—the windows of the soul, as Shakespeare called them.

Deep. A funny word to describe an action that we know can't really be deep at all. Sight is a strictly physical affair. Photons of light strike the retinal wall at the rear of the eye, a mere inch or so behind the pupil, and the information they deliver is then translated into electrochemical impulses that travel along the optic nerve to the visual processing center in the rear of the brain. It's an entirely mechanical process.

But of course, everyone knows just what you mean when you say you're looking deep into someone's eyes. You're seeing that person's soul—that part of the human being that the ancient Greek philosopher Heraclitus was talking about some 2,500 years ago when he wrote: "You would not find the limits of the soul even if you travelled forever, so deep and vast is it." Illusion or not, it is a powerful thing to glimpse that depth when it presents itself.

We see this depth manifested most powerfully on two occasions: when we fall in love, and when we see someone die. Most people have experienced the first, while fewer, in our society where death is so shunted out of sight, have experienced the second. But medical people and hospice workers who see death regularly will know immediately what I'm talking about. Suddenly where there was depth there is now only surface. The living gaze—even if the person in question was very old and that gaze was vague and flickering—goes flat.

We see this when an animal dies, too. The direct avenue into what the twentieth-century scholar of religions Titus Burckhardt called "the inward realm of the soul" goes dead, and the body becomes, in essence, like an unplugged appliance.

So imagine that bride and groom looking into each other's eyes, and seeing that bottomless depth. The shutter snaps. The image is captured. A perfect shot of a perfect pair of young newlyweds.

Now jump ahead half a dozen decades. Imagine that this couple had kids, and that those kids had kids of their own. The man in the picture has died, and the woman now lives alone in an assisted living facility. Her kids visit her, she has friends at the facility, but sometimes, like right now, she feels alone.

It's a rainy afternoon, and the woman, sitting by her window, has picked up that photo from where it sits in a frame on a side table. In the gray light filtering in, she looks at it. The photo, like the woman herself, has taken a long journey to get there. It started out in a photo album that was passed on to one of their children, then went into a frame and came with her when she moved to the facility. Though it's fragile, a little yellowed and bent at the edges, it has survived. She sees the young woman she was, looking into the eyes of her new husband, and remembers how at that moment he was more real to her than anything else in the world.

Where is he now? Does he still exist?

On good days, the woman knows he does. Surely the man she loved so much for all those many years could not have simply vanished when his body died. She knows—vaguely—what religion has to say on the matter. Her husband is off in heaven: a heaven that, through years of more or less steady church attendance, she has professed belief in. Though deep down she has never been all that sure.

So on other days—days like today—she doubts. For she also knows what science has to say on this matter. Yes, she loved her husband. But love is an emotion, an electrochemical reaction that goes on deep inside the brain, releasing hormones into the body, dictating our moods, telling us whether to be happy or sad, joyous or desolate.

In short, love is unreal.

What *is* real? Well, that's obvious. The molecules of steel and chrome and aluminum and plastic in the chair she sits in; the carbon atoms that make up the paper of the photo she holds in her hand; the glass and wood of the frame that protects it. And of course the diamond on her engagement ring and the gold of which both it and her wedding ring are made: those are real, too.

But the perfect, whole, and everlasting bond of love between two immortal souls that these rings are meant to signify? Well, that's all just pretty-sounding fluff. Solid, tangible matter: that's what's real. Science says so.

The inside is your true nature.
—AL-GHAZALI, ELEVENTH-CENTURY ISLAMIC MYSTIC

The root of the word *reality* is the Latin word *res*—"thing." The things in our lives like car tires, pans, footballs, and backyard swing sets are real to us because they possess a day-in, day-out consistency. We can touch them, weigh them in our hands, put them down, and come back later and find them unchanged, right where we left them.

We, of course, are made of matter as well. Our bodies are made of elements like hydrogen, the earliest and simplest element, and more complex ones like nitrogen, carbon, iron, and magnesium. All of these were cooked up—created—at inconceivable pressure and heat, in the hearts of ancient, now long-dead stars. Carbon nuclei have six protons and six neutrons. Of the eight positions in its outer shell where its electrons orbit, four are occupied by electrons, and four are vacant, so that electrons from other atoms or elements can link up with the carbon atom by binding their own electrons to those empty positions. This particular symmetry allows carbon atoms to link together with other carbon atoms, as well as other kinds of atoms and molecules, with fantastic efficiency. Both organic chemistry and biochemistry—massive subjects that dwarf chemistry's other subsets—are exclusively devoted to studying chemical interactions involving carbon. The entire chemical structure of life on earth is based on carbon and its unique attributes. It is the lingua franca of the organic chemical world. Thanks to this same symmetry, carbon atoms, when submitted to tremendous pressure, lock together with a new tenacity, transforming from the black, earthy stuff we associate it with into that most powerful natural symbol of durability, the diamond.

But though the atoms of carbon and the handful of other elements that make up most of our bodies are all essentially immortal, our bodies themselves are transient in the extreme. New cells are born and old ones die. At every moment our bodies are taking matter from, and giving it back to, the physical world around us. Before long—the blink of an eye on a cosmic scale—our bodies will go back into the cycle entirely. They will rejoin the flux of carbon, hydrogen, oxygen, calcium, and other primary substances that build up and disintegrate, again and again, here on earth.

This insight is nothing new, of course. The word *human*

itself comes from the same root as *humus,* earth. So too does *humble,* which makes sense because the best way of staying humble is to realize what you're made of. Long before science came along to explain the minute details of how it happens, cultures all around the world knew that our bodies are made from earth, and that when we die our bodies go back to it. As God says to Adam—a name itself derived from the Hebrew word *adamah*—"earth"—in Genesis: "Dust thou art, and to dust thou will return."

Yet we humans have never been completely happy with this situation. The whole history of humanity can be seen as our response to this apparent earthiness of ours, and the feelings of pain and incompletion that it creates. We suspect that there is something more to the story.

Modern science—the latest and by far the most powerful of our responses to this ancient restlessness about our mortality—grew in large part out of an ancient technique of manipulating chemicals called alchemy. The origins of alchemy are lost in history. Some say it began in ancient Greece. Others say the first alchemists lived much earlier, perhaps in Egypt, and that the name itself derives from the Egyptian *Al-Kemi* or "black earth"—presumably a reference to the black, fertile soil on the banks of the Nile.

There were Christian alchemists, Jewish alchemists, Muslim alchemists, and Taoist or Confucian alchemists. It was simply everywhere. Wherever and whenever it did begin, alchemy grew into a fantastically complex and widespread series of practices. Most of these were concerned with turning "base" metals like copper and lead into gold. But the prime goal of alchemy was recovering the state of immortality that the alchemists believed humankind originally possessed, but lost long ago.

Many of the tools and methods of modern chemistry were invented by alchemists, often at considerable risk. Messing around with physical matter can be dangerous, and in addition to poisoning or blowing themselves up, alchemists risked getting in trouble with the local religious powers. Like the science it gave rise to, alchemy was, especially in Europe in the years leading up to the Scientific Revolution, a heresy.

One of the major discoveries of the alchemists in the course of their quest for immortality was that when you submit a chemical or element to what alchemists called a "trying" process—if you heat it, say, or combine it with some other chemical with which it is reactive—it will turn into something else. Like so many other gifts from the past, this knowledge sounds obvious to us now, but this is only because we didn't do the work to discover it to begin with.

The first age was golden.
—OVID, *METAMORPHOSES*

Why were the alchemists so interested in gold? One reason is obvious. The lesser alchemists—those who didn't understand the deeper, underlying spiritual element at work in it—were simply trying to become rich. But the real alchemists were interested in gold for another reason.

Gold, like carbon, is an unusual element. The nucleus of the gold atom is very large. With seventy-nine protons, only four other stable elements are heavier. This big positive electrical charge causes the electrons that circle the nucleus of the gold atom to move at exceptional speed—approximately half the speed of light. If a photon comes to earth from the sun, the heavenly body most associated with gold in the alchemical texts, and bounces off an atom of gold, and that photon then happens to enter into one of our eyes and strikes the retinal wall, the message this delivers to the brain creates a curiously pleasant sensation in our consciousness. We humans react strongly to gold, and always have.

Gold powers much of the economic activity on our planet. It is beautiful and it is relatively rare, yet it has no great utilitarian value—nothing like the one we have placed on it, in any case. We have, as a species, *decided* it has value; that's all. That's why alchemists, both through their material experiments and the inner, meditative practices that often accompanied those experiments, sought it so desperately. Gold, for them, was the solidified, tangible representation of the heavenly part of the human being—the immortal soul. They sought to recover that other side of the human being—the golden side that joins with the earthy side to make us the people we are.

We are one part earth and one part heaven, and the alchemists knew this.

We need to know it, too.

Qualities, like the "beauty" of gold, and even its very color, are, we have been taught, not real. Emotions, we have been taught, are even less real. They're just reactive patterns generated by our brains in response to hormonal messages sent by our bodies in response to situations of danger or desire.

Love. Beauty. Goodness. Friendship. In the worldview of materialist science, there is no room for treating these things as realities. When we believe this, just as when we believe it when we are told that meaning isn't real, we lose our connection to heaven—what writers in the ancient world sometimes called the "golden thread."

We get weak.

Love, beauty, goodness, and friendship are real. They're as real as rain. They're as real as butter, as real as wood, or stone, or plutonium, or the rings of Saturn, or sodium nitrate. On the earthly level of existence, it's easy to lose sight of that.

But what you lose, you can get back.

Unlettered peoples are ignorant of many things, but they are seldom stupid because, having to rely on their memories, they are more likely to remember what is important. Literate peoples, by contrast, are apt to get lost in their vast libraries of recorded information.[*]

—HUSTON SMITH, RELIGION SCHOLAR

---

[*] Smith, *The Way Things Are*, 79.

Human beings have been around in our modern form for about one hundred thousand years. For most of this time, three questions have been intensely important to us:

Who are we?

Where did we come from?

Where are we going?

For the vast majority of our time on this planet, human beings didn't doubt for a moment that the spiritual world was real. We believed that it was the place each of us came from when we were born, and that it was the place we would return to when we died.

Many scientists today think we are right on the verge of knowing just about everything there is to know about the universe. There is much talk these days, among certain of these scientists, of a "Theory of Everything." A theory that will account for every last bit of data about the universe that we currently possess: a theory that, as the name suggests, will explain it all.

But there's something rather curious about this theory. It doesn't include answers to a single one of those three questions listed above: the questions that, for 99.9 percent of our time on earth, were the three most important ones to answer. This Theory of Everything makes no mention of heaven.

The word *heaven* originally meant, simply, "sky." That is what the word that translates as "heaven" in the New Testament means. The Spanish word for heaven, *cielo*, also means "sky," and comes from the same root that our word *ceiling* does as well. Though we now know that heaven isn't *literally* up there, many of us continue to sense that there is a dimension or dimensions that are "above" the earthly world in the sense that they are "higher" in a spiritual sense. When I use "heaven" in this book, and talk about it being "above" us, I am doing so with the understanding that no one today thinks heaven is simply up there in the sky, or that it is the simple place of clouds and eternal sunshine that the word has come to conjure up. I am speaking in terms of another kind of geography: one that is very real, but also very different from the earthly one we are familiar with, and in comparison to which the entire observable physical dimension is as a grain of sand on a beach.

There is another group out there today—a group that also includes many scientists—that also believes we might indeed be on the verge of discovering a Theory of Everything. But the Theory of Everything that this group is talking about is quite different from the one that materialist science thinks it's on the verge of discovering.

This other theory will be different from the first one in two major ways.

The first is that it will posit that we can't ever really *have* a Theory of Everything, if by that we mean an aggressive, materialist, data-oriented one.

The second difference is that, in this other Theory of Everything, all three of those original, all-important primordial questions about the human condition will be addressed. Heaven will be included in it.

Introduction

*I regard consciousness as fundamental. I regard matter
as derivative from consciousness. We cannot get behind
consciousness. Everything that we talk about, everything
that we regard as existing, postulates consciousness.*
—MAX PLANCK (1858–1947), QUANTUM PHYSICIST

In the twentieth century, after three fantastically successful centuries, science—in particular, the branch of science
known as physics—got a surprise. Deep down, at the very
heart of matter, it found something it couldn't explain. It
turned out that "matter," that stuff that science thought it
understood so well, wasn't what science had thought it was at
all. Atoms—those unbreakable, rock-solid little objects that
science had thought were the ultimate building blocks of the
world—turned out to be not so solid, or so unbreakable, after
all. Matter turned out to be a dazzlingly intricate matrix of
super-powerful but nonmaterial forces. There was nothing
material *to* it.

It got even weirder. If there was one thing that science
thought it knew as well as matter, it was space—the area that
matter moved around in, nice and simple. But space wasn't
really "there," either. At least not in the simple, straightfor-
ward, easy-to-understand way that scientists had thought it
was. It bent. It stretched. It was inextricably linked with time.
It was anything but simple.

Then, as if that weren't enough, another factor entered into the picture: a factor that science had long known about, but had up until then displayed no interest in. In fact, science had only coined a word for this phenomenon in the seventeenth century, even though the world's prescientific peoples all placed it at the center of their view of reality and had dozens of words for it.

This new factor was consciousness—that simple, yet supremely unsimple fact of being aware—of knowing oneself and the world around one.

No one in the scientific community had the remotest idea what consciousness was, but this hadn't been a problem before. Scientists just left it out of the picture—because, they said, being unmeasurable, consciousness wasn't real. But in the 1920s, quantum mechanical experiments revealed not only that you *could* detect consciousness, but that, at a subatomic level, there was no way of *not* doing so, because the consciousness of the observer actually bound the observer to all he or she observed. It was an irremovable part of any scientific experiment.

This was a staggering revelation—despite the fact that most scientists still chose, by and large, to ignore it. Much to the chagrin of the many scientists who believed they were right on the edge of explaining everything in the universe from a completely materialistic perspective, consciousness now moved right to the center of the stage and refused to be pushed aside. As the years went on and scientific experimentation at the subatomic level—a domain known, in general, as quantum mechanics—became ever more sophisticated, the key role that consciousness played in every experiment became ever clearer, if still impossible to explain. As the Hungarian-American theoretical physicist Eugene Wigner wrote: "It was not possible to formulate the laws of quantum mechanics in a fully consistent way without reference to consciousness." The Spanish mathematical physicist Ernst Pascual Jordan put the matter even more forcefully: "Observations," he wrote, "not only disturb what is to be measured, they produce it." This doesn't necessarily mean that we make reality with our imaginations; but it does mean that consciousness is so tied up with reality that there is no way of conceiving reality without it. Consciousness is the true bedrock of existence.

The physics community has yet to interpret what the results of experiments in quantum mechanics reveal about the workings of the universe. The brilliant founding fathers of the field, including Werner Heisenberg, Louis de Broglie, Sir James Jeans, Erwin Schrödinger, Wolfgang Pauli, and Max Planck, were driven into mysticism in their efforts to fully comprehend the results of their experiments about the workings of the subatomic world. According to the "measurement problem," consciousness plays a crucial role in determining the nature of evolving reality. There is no way to separate the observer from the observed. The reality portrayed by experiments in quantum mechanics is completely counterintuitive from what one might expect based on our daily lives in the earthly realm. A deeper understanding and interpretation will require a thorough reworking of our concepts of consciousness, causality, space, and time. In fact, a robust enhancement of physics that fully embraces the reality of consciousness (soul or spirit) as the basis of *all that is* will be necessary to transcend the profound enigma at the heart of quantum physics.

I maintain that the human mystery is incredibly demeaned by scientific reductionism, with its claim in promissory materialism to account eventually for all of the spiritual world in terms of patterns of neuronal activity. This belief must be classed as a superstition. . . . we have to recognize that we are spiritual beings with souls existing in a spiritual world as well as material beings with bodies and brains existing in a material world.

— SIR JOHN C. ECCLES (1903–1997), NEUROPHYSIOLOGIST

No description of the nature of reality can even begin before we have a much clearer view of the true nature of consciousness, and its relationship to emerging reality in the physical realm. We could make greater progress if those trained in physics would also jump headlong into the study of what some scientists have called the "hard problem of consciousness." The essence of the hard problem is that modern neuroscience assumes that the brain creates consciousness out of its sheer complexity. However, there is absolutely no explanation that suggests any mechanism by which this occurs. In fact, the more research we do on the brain, the more we realize that consciousness exists independently of it. Roger Penrose, Henry Stapp, Amit Goswami, and Brian Josephson are notable examples of physicists who have pursued an incorporation of consciousness into physics models, but most of the physics community remains oblivious to the more esoteric levels of inquiry required.

The day science begins to study nonphysical phenomena,
it will make more progress in one decade than in all the
previous centuries of its existence.
—NIKOLA TESLA (1856–1943)

The new theory—the new "Map of Everything" that I am so in favor of—will include all the revolutionary discoveries that science has made in the last century, most especially the new discoveries about the nature of matter and space and the revolutionary discoveries of the centrality of consciousness that threw materialistic science into such chaos at the beginning of the twentieth century. It will address discoveries like that of the physicist Werner Heisenberg that subatomic particles are never actually in one place, but occupy a constant state of statistical probability—so that they might be here, or they might be there, but they can never be totally nailed down to a single, no-doubt-about-it spot. Or that a photon—a unit of light—will appear as a wave if we measure it in one way, and as a particle if we measure it in another way, *even while remaining exactly the same photon*. Or discoveries like Erwin Schrödinger's that the outcome of certain subatomic experiments will be determined by the consciousness of the observer recording them in such a way that they can actually "reverse" time, so that an atomic reaction set off inside a box that was sealed three days previously will not actually complete itself until the box is opened and the results of the action are noted by a conscious observer. The atomic reaction stays in a suspended state of both happening and not happening until consciousness enters the picture and cements it into reality.

This new Map of Everything will also include the vast quantities of data that are coming in from a whole other area of research, one that materialist science paid even less attention to in the past than it did to consciousness, and that dogmatic religion resolutely ignored as well: Near-death experiences. Deathbed visions. Moments of apparent contact with departed loved ones. The whole world of strange but totally real encounters with the spiritual world that people experience all the time, but that neither dogmatic science nor dogmatic religion has allowed us to talk about.

The kind of events that people talk to *me* about all the time.

Dear Dr. Alexander,

I loved reading about your experience. It reminded me of my father's near death experience four years before he passed away.

Introduction

*My dad had a PhD in astrophysics and was absolutely 100%
"scientifically minded" before his near death experience.*

*He was in a pretty bad way in intensive care. He had trodden
an emotionally hard path in life and fallen prey to alcoholism,
until many of his body organs packed up and he caught double
pneumonia. He was in intensive care for three months. During
that time, he spent a while in an induced coma. When he started
to recover he began to relay his experience of being with angel-
like beings who were communicating to him not to worry and
that everything was going to be fine. They said he would get
better and continue his life. He said they were helping him and
that he was no longer afraid of dying. He used to tell me, after
he recovered, not to worry when he did die and to know that he
would be fine.*

*. . . [H]e changed massively after his experience. He didn't
drink anymore, but . . . speaking about it was too much for
him . . . he was a very private man. . . . He died of a tear in
his aorta very suddenly at home in his sleep, four years after
his stay in hospital. We kept finding Post-It notes around his
house after he died—"GaHf." In the end, we deduced it to mean
"Guardian angels. Have faith." Maybe this had helped him in
his abstinence. It maybe helped him to remember the comfort he
had felt while out of his body.*

*Soon before he died I remember asking him what he thought
happens when we actually die. He said he didn't really know,
and that it was just something that we as humans haven't
found out yet, but we will. I guess he had experienced the place
where science and spirituality meet. It was a real comfort*

*to read your experience and it reaffirmed to me my dad's
experience too.*

Many thanks,
Pascale

Why do people tell me stories like this? The answer is
simple. I'm a doctor who had an NDE—a solid member of
the "dogmatic science" side of the room, who had an experience that sent him over to the other side. Not the "dogmatic
religion" side, but a third side of the room, if you will: a side
that believes science and religion both have things to teach
us, but that neither has, or ever will, have all the answers. This
side of the room believes that we are on the edge of something
genuinely new: a marriage of spirituality and science that
will change the way we understand and experience ourselves
forever.

In *Proof of Heaven,* I described how the sudden onset of a
very rare strain of bacterial meningitis put me in a hospital,
and a deep coma, for seven days. During that time, I underwent an experience that I am still in the process of absorbing
and comprehending. I journeyed through a series of supra-
physical realms, each one more extraordinary than the last.

In the first, which I call the Realm of the Earthworm's-
Eye View, I was immersed in a primitive, primordial state of
consciousness that felt, while I was in it, something like being
buried in earth. It was, however, not ordinary earth, for all
around me I sensed—and sometimes heard and saw—other
forms, other entities. It was part horrific, part comforting

(I felt like I was, and always had been, a part of this primitive murk). I am often asked, "Was this hell?" I would expect hell to be at least a little bit interactive, and this was nothing of the sort. Even though I didn't remember earth, or even what a human was, I at least had a sense of curiosity. I would ask, "Who? What? Where?" and there was never a flicker of response.

Eventually, a being of light—a circular entity that gave off a beautiful, heavenly music that I called the Spinning Melody—came slowly down from above, throwing off marvelous filaments of living silver and golden light. The light opened up like a rip in the fabric of that coarse realm, and I felt myself going through the rip, like a portal, up into a staggeringly beautiful valley full of lush and fertile greenery, where waterfalls flowed into crystal pools. I found myself as a speck of awareness on a butterfly wing among pulsing swarms of millions of other butterflies. I witnessed stunning blue-black velvety skies filled with swooping orbs of golden light, which I later called angelic choirs, leaving sparkling trails against billowing, colorful clouds. Those choirs produced hymns and anthems far beyond anything I had ever encountered on earth. There was also a vast array of larger universes that took the form of what I came to call an "over-sphere," that was there to help in imparting the lessons I was to learn. The angelic choirs provided yet another portal to higher realms. I ascended until I reached the Core, that deepest *sanctum sanctorum* of the Divine—infinite inky blackness, filled to overflowing with indescribable divine unconditional love. There I encountered the infinitely powerful, all-knowing deity whom I later called Om, because of the sound I sensed so prominently in that realm. I learned lessons of a depth and beauty entirely beyond my capacity to explain. Throughout my time in the Core, there was always the strong sense of there being three of us (the infinite Divine, the brilliant orb, and pure conscious awareness).

During this voyage, I had a guide. She was an extraordinarily beautiful woman who first appeared as I rode, as that speck of awareness, on the wing of that butterfly in the Gateway Realm. I'd never seen this woman before. I didn't know who she was. Yet her presence was enough to heal my heart, to make me whole in a way I'd never known was possible. Without actually speaking, she let me know that I was loved and cared for beyond measure and that the universe was a vaster, better, and more beautiful place than I could ever have dreamed. I was an irreplaceable part of the whole (like all of us), and all the sadness and fear I had ever known in the past was a result of my somehow having forgotten this most central of facts.

Dear Dr. Alexander,

Thirty-four years ago I had a NDE—but it wasn't me who was dying. My mother was. She was being treated for cancer at the hospital and the doctors there told us she had at most six months to live. It was Saturday, and I was set to fly from Ohio to New Jersey on Monday. I was out in my garden, when suddenly this feeling went through me. It was overwhelming. It was a feeling of an unbelievable amount of love. It was the best "high" you could possibly imagine. I stood up, wondering: What on earth was that? Then it went through me again. It happened three times in all. I knew my mother had passed. The feeling was like she was hugging me but going right through me. And every time she did, I felt this supernatural, unbelievable, immeasurable amount of love.

I went into my house, still in a fog as to what had happened. I sat down by the phone to wait for the call from my sister. After ten minutes the phone rang. It was my sister. "Mom passed away," she said.

Even 30 years later I can't tell this story without crying—not from sadness so much as joy. Those three moments in the garden changed my life for good. Since then, I haven't feared death. I'm actually jealous of people who have passed away. (I know that sounds weird but it's true.)

Back when this happened we didn't have all these TV shows and books about NDEs. They weren't the public phenomenon they are today. So I had no idea of what to think of it. But I knew it was real.

Jean Hering

When I returned from my journey (a miracle in itself, described in detail in *Proof of Heaven*), I was in many ways like a newborn child. I had no memories of my earthly life, but knew full well where I had been. I had to relearn who, what, and where I was. Over days, then weeks, like a gently falling snow, my old, earthly knowledge came back. Words and language returned within hours and days. With the love and gentle coaxing of my family and friends, other memories came back. I returned to the human community. By eight weeks my prior knowledge of science, including the experiences and learning from more than two decades spent as a neurosurgeon in teaching hospitals, returned—completely. That full recovery remains a miracle without any explanation from modern medicine.

But I was a different person from the one I had been. The things I had seen and experienced while gone from my body did not fade away, as dreams and hallucinations do. They stayed. And the longer they stayed, the more I realized that what had happened to me in the week I spent beyond my physical body had rewritten everything I thought I knew about all of existence. The image of the woman on the butterfly wing stayed with me, haunting me, just as did all the other extraordinary things I'd encountered in those worlds beyond.

Four months after coming out of my coma, I received a picture in the mail. A photograph of my biological sister Betsy—a sister I'd never known because I had been adopted at a young age and Betsy had died before I had sought out and reunited with my biological family. The photo was of Betsy. But it was also of someone else. It was the woman on the butterfly wing.

The moment I realized this, something crystallized inside me. It was almost as if, since coming back, my mind and soul had been like the amorphous contents of a butterfly chrysalis:

I could not return to what I had been before, but I could not move forward, either. I was stuck.

That photo—as well as the sudden shock of recognition I felt when I gazed at it—was the confirmation that I'd needed. From then on, I was back in the old, earthly world I'd left behind before my coma struck, but as a genuinely new person.

I had been reborn.

But the real journey was just beginning. More is revealed to me every day—through meditation, through my work with new technologies that I hope will make it easier for others to gain access to the spiritual realm (see the appendix), and through talking with people I meet on my travels. Many, many people have glimpsed some of what I glimpsed, and experienced what I experienced. These people love to share their stories with me, and I love to hear them. It strikes them as wonderful that a long-standing member of the materialist scientific community could be changed as much as I have been. And I agree.

As a doctor with a long career at esteemed medical institutions like Duke and Harvard, I was the perfect understanding skeptic. I was the guy who, if you told me about your NDE, or the visit you'd received from your dead aunt to tell you that all was well with her, would have looked at you and said, sympathetically but definitively, that it was a fantasy.

Countless people are having experiences like these. I meet them every day. Not just at the talks I give, but standing behind me in line at Starbucks and sitting next to me on airplanes. I have become, through the reach that *Proof of Heaven* achieved, someone whom people feel they can talk to about this kind of thing. When they do, I am always astonished at the remarkable unity and coherence of what they have to say. I am discovering more and more similarities between what these people tell me and what the peoples of the past believed. I am discovering what the ancients knew well: Heaven makes us human. We forget it at our peril. Without knowledge of the larger geography of where we came from and where we are going again when our physical bodies die, we are lost. That "golden thread" is the connection to the above that makes life here below not just tolerable but joyful. We are lost without it.

My story is a piece of the puzzle—a further hint from the universe and the loving God at work in it that the time of bossy science and bossy religion is over, and that a new marriage of the better, deeper parts of the scientific and spiritual sensibilities is going to occur at last.

In this book, I share what I have learned from others— ancient philosophers and mystics, modern scientists, and many, many ordinary people like me—about what I call the Gifts of Heaven. These gifts are the benefits that come when we open ourselves to the single greatest truth that those before us knew: there is a larger world behind the one we see around us every day. That larger world loves us more than we can possibly imagine. It is watching us at every moment, hoping that we will see hints in the world around us that it is there, as depicted in the following account given to Alistair Hardy during his investigations into spiritual experiences (pg.67).

Introduction

*For a few seconds only, I suppose, the whole compartment was
filled with light. This is the only way I know in which to describe
the moment, for there was nothing to see at all. I felt caught up
into some tremendous sense of being within a loving, triumphant
and shining purpose. I never felt more humble. I never felt more
exalted. A most curious but overwhelming sense possessed me and
filled me with ecstasy. I felt that all was well for mankind—how
poor the words seem! The word "well" is so poverty stricken. All
men were shining and glorious beings who in the end would
enter incredible joy. Beauty, music, joy, love immeasurable and a
glory unspeakable, all this they would inherit. Of this they were
heirs.*

*All this happened over fifty years ago but even now I can
see myself in the corner of that dingy, third-class compartment
with the feeble lights of inverted gas mantles overhead. . . . In a
few moments the glory departed—all but one curious, lingering
feeling. I loved everybody in that compartment. It sounds silly
now, and indeed I blush to write it, but at that moment I think I
would have died for any one of the people in that compartment.**

My whole life has been a search for belonging. Growing up
the son of a highly respected brain surgeon, I was constantly
aware of the admiration-bordering-on-veneration that people
have for surgeons. People worshipped my dad. Not that he
encouraged it. A humble man with a strong Christian faith,

---

*Religious Experience Research Center, account number 000385, quoted in Hardy, *The
Spiritual Nature of Man*, 53.

Introduction

he treated his responsibility as a healer with far too much weight to ever indulge in self-aggrandizement. I marveled at his humility and his deep sense of his own calling. I wanted nothing more than to be like him; to measure up; to become a member of the medical brotherhood that, in my eyes, had a sacred allure.

After years of hard work, I earned my way deep into that secular brother and sisterhood of surgeons. However, the spiritual faith that had come so easily and naturally to my father evaded me. Like many other surgeons in the modern world, I was a master of the physical side of the human being, and a complete innocent about the spiritual side. I simply didn't believe it existed.

Then came my NDE, in 2008. What happened to me is an illustration of what is happening to us as a culture at large, as is each individual story I have heard from the people I've met. Each of us carries a memory of heaven, buried deep within us. Bringing that memory to the surface—helping you find your own map to that very real place—is the purpose of this book.

The MAP of HEAVEN

CHAPTER I

The Gift of Knowledge

*Every man is born an Aristotelian or a Platonist.**
— SAMUEL TAYLOR COLERIDGE (1772–1834)

Plato and Aristotle are the two fathers of the Western world. Plato (c. 428–c. 348 BCE) is the father of religion and philosophy, and Aristotle (384–322 BCE) is the father of science. Plato was Aristotle's teacher, but Aristotle ended up disagreeing with much of what Plato had to say. Specifically, Aristotle questioned Plato's assertion that there is a spiritual world beyond the earthly one: a world infinitely more real, upon which all that we experience in this world is based.

Plato did more than just believe in that larger world. He went within, and he could *feel* it there inside him. Plato was

---

* *Specimens of the Table Talk of the Late Samuel Taylor Coleridge*, entry for July 2, 1830 (1835).

a mystic, and like countless mystics before and after him, he realized that his consciousness, his inner self, was intimately connected to this larger world of spirit. He was, to use a modern analogy, hooked up to it. The juice of heaven flowed inside him.

Aristotle was built differently. He did not feel that direct connection to the living spiritual world that Plato did. To Aristotle, Plato's world of Forms—the trans-earthly, super-physical structures that Plato felt all the objects in our world were mere dim reflections of—was a fantasy. Where was the proof of these magical entities, and the spiritual world to which Plato said they belonged? For Aristotle as for Plato, the world was a keenly, wonderfully intelligent place. But the root of that intelligence and order did not lie off in some great Beyond. It was all right down here, in front of us.

Though they disagreed often, there was also much that Plato and Aristotle agreed on. One of their deepest points of consensus was their concept of what one might call the reasonableness of the world—the fact that life can be understood. Behind the modern word *logic* lies the Greek word *logos*—a term that we know today largely through Christianity, where it is another term for the being of Christ as the Word of God made manifest. In Plato and Aristotle's time, it meant the living intelligence at work in the physical world and in the human mind. It was the *logos* that allowed humans to understand the order of the world, for—as both Plato and Aristotle believed—we can understand the world because we are of a piece with it. Geometry, number, logic, rhetoric, medicine—all of these disciplines, and the others that Plato and Aristotle helped to develop, are possible because human beings are built to understand the world they live in.

What we call learning is only a process of recollection.
—PLATO

Aristotle was the first great mapper of earthly order. His political writings celebrate the idea that human beings do not need trans-earthly inspiration to discover the best way to live and govern. We can do it ourselves. The answers to the big questions, and the smaller ones, too, are right here on earth, waiting to be uncovered.

Plato felt differently. Among his other distinctions, Plato is the father of the Western near-death narrative. In *The Republic*, Plato tells the story of an Armenian soldier named Er. Wounded in battle and mistaken for dead, Er was placed on a funeral pyre. He revived just before the flames were lit, and told a story of going to a realm beyond the earth—a beautiful place where souls were judged for the good or bad they'd done while here.

It was a story Plato found deeply significant. He believed we come to earth from this place above, the place that Er visited in his NDE, and that if we look deep within, we can recover memories of our existence there. These memories, if we trust and build on them, can create an unshakable orientation. They can keep us anchored, while we are here on earth, to the celestial earth above from which we came. To use a wonderful Greek word, we have to perform an act of *anamnesis*—a word that translates as "remembrance." The key to understanding this world and living well while here on earth is to remember the place above and beyond, where we really came from.

Plato lived at a time when the earth was thought to be a flat disk with Greece at its center, and around which the heavens circled in orderly fashion. Today we live in a universe 93 billion light-years wide, 13.7 billion years old, on a planet circling an average "G2"-type star some 875,000 miles across, in a barred spiral galaxy containing some 300 billion other stars—a planet that is some 4.54 billion years old, on which life appeared 3.8 billion years ago, and on which the first roughly hominid creatures arrived about a million years ago.

We know much, much more about the universe than Plato or Aristotle did.

And yet from another perspective, we know a good deal less.

One of Plato's most famous stories concerns a group of people in a dark cave. The people are chained in such a way that they can see only the wall in front of them. There is a fire behind them, and they can see shadows playing on the wall: shadows cast by the light of the fire on shapes that their captors, standing behind them, hold up and move about.

These flickering shadows constitute this people's entire world. Even if these people were unchained and let out into the real light of day, the light would so blind them, Plato suggests, that they would not know what to make of what they saw.

It's plain enough whom Plato is really talking about in this elaborate but striking story.

Us.

Anyone who has read Plato or Aristotle knows that their arguments are far from simple, and slicing them down the middle like this does their subtlety and complexity an injustice. But the distinction between these two philosophers is very real all the same, and it has had a profound effect on us. Their ideas have a direct effect on how you and I experience the world every day. Plato and Aristotle made us who we are. If you live in the modern world, you absorbed their lessons long before you were old enough to realize you were doing so. For the fact is, we are all metaphysicians. The most down-to-earth, unmetaphysical person in the world has a vast set of metaphysical assumptions about the world running every second. Our choice is not whether or not to be interested in philosophical questions, but whether or not to become conscious of the fact that, as human beings, we can't help but be.

To understand the world that Plato and Aristotle came from—and hence the world we live in today—we need to know a little about the mystery religions, which played a huge role in the ancient Mediterranean for a thousand years before Plato, Aristotle, and the other originators of modern thought came along. Plato was an initiate in at least one of these religions, and what he learned in them informed everything he wrote. Aristotle's membership is more doubtful, but he was deeply influenced by them as well, as many of his writings, especially those on drama, demonstrate.

There is much argument about how much or how little the mystery religions informed the attitudes of Jesus and the first Christians. The rite of baptism is shared with the mysteries, along with the concept of a god (or goddess) who dies and comes back to life, and in doing so redeems the world. The mysteries, like Christianity, placed a great emphasis on initiation—on the transformation of their members as beings of earth into beings of earth and starry heaven.

These kinds of rites existed everywhere in the past, not just Greece. They were a central part of what it meant to be human. Most often they occurred around adolescence, when a young man or woman attained physical maturity, or later on, when an individual entered into the trade or skill that would occupy and define much of his or her life from then on. All of them had one chief goal: reawakening our spiritual memory of who and what we are, where we came from, and where we're going.

In the mystery religions, as in most ancient initiations, the person being initiated died as the earthly person he or she had been, and was reborn as a new, spiritual one. Not in some vague, theoretical way, but for real. The central concept of the mysteries, as of most ancient initiatory practices, was that as humans we have a dual heritage: an earthly one and a heavenly one. To know only one's earthly heritage is to know only half of oneself. The mystery initiations allowed people to recover a direct knowledge of what we could call their "heavenly" lineage. In a sense, the initiate wasn't turned into anything new so much as he or she was reminded, in a powerful and immediate way, of who and what he or she had started out as before coming to earth, of what he or she really had been all along.

The Eleusinian mysteries, named after the Greek city of Eleusis where they took place, were the most renowned of these rites. They were based on the myth of Persephone, a girl who was abducted by Hades, the god of the underworld, and taken down into his kingdom. Persephone's mother, Demeter, was so heartbroken at losing her that she eventually struck a deal with Hades, so that Persephone would spend half the year in the underworld, and the other half of the year on the surface of the earth. The half that Persephone spent down in the underworld was winter. Consequently, the life of the rivers and fields left with her in autumn, then returned in spring, bursting out in the form of new plant and animal life.

Persephone is related to a much older goddess named Inanna, who was worshipped by the Sumerians—a people who lived several thousand years earlier than the Greeks, in the Fertile Crescent, the area that would later give rise to the Israelites. Inanna was the Queen of Heaven, and the central myth the Sumerians told about her concerned her descent into the land of the dead. The myth tells us that on her way down she passed through seven levels of the underworld, removing a different garment or ornament at each level until she stood naked before the Lord of Death—who was also, as it happens, her sister. Inanna was killed and hung on a hook against a wall. But, much like Persephone, she revived and returned to earth. Her triumph was not complete, however, because the Sumerians viewed death not just as a foe, but also as an essentially unconquerable one.

Though built in part around these ancient myths, the mysteries tell a story with a different ending. Rather incredibly, given the fact that they lasted more than a thousand years, we still don't know exactly what happened in the mysteries. We do know they could be intensely dramatic, and sometimes climaxed with the initiate being shown an object: sometimes something as mundane as a spear of wheat. The initiate was prepared for this moment through a slow and steady dramatic buildup that might have included rhythmic music, dancing, and, in the last sections of the rite, being led blindfolded into an inner sanctum where the ultimate secrets were revealed. Thanks to this carefully orchestrated preparation, this climactic vision had not only a profound symbolic significance for the initiate but a very real psychic and emotional one as well. The initiate saw the symbolic object revealed to him or her as more than an ordinary, worldly object but as an actual living window into the world beyond. If a spear of wheat was held up to the initiate, for example, it was not just a symbol of the fact that the crops die and return each year, but an actual demonstration of the core truth that the mysteries were all about: death is followed by rebirth. Gazing on it in his or her heightened state of anticipation, the initiate saw it as a dazzling, confirmatory emblem of the fact that he or she too had now been initiated into eternal life. We do not die at death.

A person who had been initiated into the mysteries was,

it was said, like a newborn child, which is why initiates were often called "twice born." They had seen a reality that was *more real* than the reality of earth, and that created in them an unshakable certainty that human life continued beyond death. This certainty went so deep that from then on, whatever happiness or sadness life brought with it, there was a part of the initiate that was simply *never* sad. It couldn't be, because the initiate had recovered through direct experience the knowledge of who we are, where we came from, and where we're going. From then on, the initiate was a dual citizen: one who even while still in this world already had one foot in a glorious, light-filled beyond.

Maybe you're starting to get a hint of the other reason I'm bringing these ancient ideas into this book. If you read *Proof of Heaven*, you probably already noticed a few familiar echoes of my story in those myths above. Why the similarities? What do they mean? I believe that we are hankering for the truths that the mysteries and the other initiatory traditions taught to people in the ancient world, and that Christianity, perhaps most especially in its beginnings, also taught (a fact I believe both Christians and non-Christians can appreciate, because these truths transcend all the dogmas and differences that so tear the world today). I believe that heaven makes us human, that without a knowledge that it is where we come from and where we're going—that it is our true country—life makes no sense. And I believe that the experiences so many people have shared with me are reminders that we need to know these truths every bit as much today as we ever did in the past.

The Map of Heaven

Dear Dr. Alexander,

. . . The one thing that troubles me is your "Earthworm Period"
which I find terrifying. I cannot help but wonder why you
experienced that and if you have found others who did as well.
I cannot seem to fit that into my "worldview." I hope you will
address it in a future publication.

I have decided to train to work as a hospice volunteer so that I
might in addition to perhaps providing a little comfort to people
who are dying, learn more about what we might call that event
horizon.

Death: It is the greatest adventure. It is stunning that in
western civilization we deny it to the degree that we do. Perhaps
that goes a long way toward explaining our societal dysfunction.

The ancient Greeks loved life. The *Iliad* and the *Odyssey*
both vibrate with the joys and pains of physical existence.
But the Greeks of Homer's time, some five hundred years
before Plato and Aristotle, did not believe in heaven. When
they thought of the afterlife, they thought of a pale, ghostly
world of phantoms: a place a lot worse, and a lot less, than this
world. Better a slave in this world, the character Achilles says
in Homer's *Odyssey*, than a king in the afterworld.

A lot of ancient peoples thought of the afterlife this way,
and it seems that rites like the mysteries evolved as a response
to this universal human fear that the afterlife was grim and
murky. Death has always been terrifying, and ancient peoples
knew this even better than most of us today do, as they saw

death at close range every day. The mystery traditions are a good example of the way many peoples around the world have dealt with death. Death could be feared back then. It could be railed against or joyously accepted. But it could not be simply ignored.

"Happy is he who has seen this," says one mystery text of the initiate who has seen through the terrors of death to the wonders lying beyond. "Who has not taken part in the initiation will not have the same lot after death in the gloomy darkness."* That gray, grim realm bears more than a little similarity to where I started out on my journey: that elemental, mud-like "place" that in *Proof of Heaven* I call the Realm of the Earthworm's-Eye View.

It is not always easy to navigate the many realms that exist beyond the body. The Realm of the Earthworm's-Eye View, as I experienced it, was not a place of fear or punishment: it was not someplace that you were "sent" for not behaving properly. But I have now discovered that it bears a great resemblance to the dim, swampy, lower areas of the afterlife as described by many ancient societies.

The realm of soul is like an ocean. It's vast. When the physical body and brain, which act as buffers for this world while we are alive, fall away, we risk falling into the lower realms of the spiritual world: realms that correspond directly to the lower portions of our psyche and are, as such, murky in the extreme. That, I believe, is what the ancients were talking

---

*From the *Homeric Hymns*, http://www.sacred-texts.com/cla/gpr/gpr07.htm.

about whenever they brought up realms of afterlife that were grim, dark, and miserable. And that's why initiation was so important, both in Greece and in so many other ancient cultures. Through initiations, people were reminded experientially of their true identities as cosmic beings whose inner structure directly mirrored the structure of the spiritual worlds that waited at death. The idea that the human soul is modeled on the spiritual worlds meant that by following the ancient Greek injunction to "know thyself," one learned to know the cosmos that gave us birth as well. Initiations were often frightening in parts because the spiritual world has its darker areas, just as the human psyche does. But mostly these rites appear to have been deeply affirming. The initiates knew that the rites they had experienced had prepared them both to bear the burdens of earthly life and to find their way back home to the higher regions of the world beyond when they reentered it at death. These were *realities* for these ancient peoples. What they had to say about them was based at least in some part on experience, which is why their writings on these subjects can be thrilling and, for some people, terrifying.

But there is no need to fear. Once free of the buffering system that our physical brains and bodies provide, we will make it to where we belong. Even if we are not perfect (and I know a little about this because I certainly am not) we will make it to that realm of light and love and acceptance. It is not about being a saint, not about being perfect (which, on a deep spiritual level, we are now, already). But it *is*, I believe, about being open. Open enough to allow ourselves to be pulled from the realms of darkness in the afterlife, which correspond to the sea of our own darker, dimmer regions, up into those regions of light that we all have the ability to enter if we want to.

I was rescued, I believe, because once out of my physical body I was open enough to be ready to say yes to the Spinning Melody and the light that came from it when it came down and opened the portal to the higher realms. It offered to be my guide, and it did not take long for me to wordlessly say yes to its invitation to follow it up into the world of light. That part of me reacted with joy and relief and recognition when, with its radiant filaments of gold, it came down to "get" me. But there are people who are not open to that good, when it comes for them. When that light descends, nothing in them says yes to it. So they stay where they are—in the dark—until they are ready to be brought out of it. Knowing this ahead of time is invaluable. That's why, for the ancients, knowledge of the existence of the worlds beyond, and of what they looked like, was one of the greatest gifts of heaven.

CHAPTER 2

The Gift of Meaning

More than anything else, the future of civilization depends on the way the two most powerful forces of history, science and religion, settle into relationship with each other.*
—ALFRED NORTH WHITEHEAD (1861–1947), PHILOSOPHER

In the spirit of the mystery religions in which he himself was an initiate, Plato turned the Homeric philosophy of the afterlife, which generally believed that that grim, gray region was all that people could hope for, on its head. Far from being a diminishment, a falling away from the brightness and sunshine and joy of earthly life, the world beyond, when we reach its higher shores, is entirely more real, more vivid, and more alive than this one. What waits beyond death, Plato argued, is

---

*Quoted in Russell, *From Science to God.*

the real world, and all life in this world is only a preparation for it. Hence his famous maxim that all true philosophy is "a preparation for death."

Plato is talking directly to us when he says this. Unlike his teacher Socrates, who like Jesus left no written words behind, Plato believed in the value of writing: of saving important ideas in written words, not just in memory, so that the forgetful people of future ages might learn again what they really need to know. The truths of the mystery religions needed new forms of expression. He saw, or thought he saw, where things were going. Like all the great spiritual teachers, he believed that the truth is meant to be shared. (Like Jesus and many another spiritual teacher, he also had his doubts about people's ability to listen.) Through his writings, Plato was giving us the answers to those three big questions we listed at the start of the book. He was setting them down quite deliberately, so that those who came after would not lose them. It is perhaps not an overstatement to say that he was trying to save them for us.

But—and this is a big reason why, as a scientist, I find his story so compelling—Plato needed Aristotle to make his message complete. By saying, in effect, that death is better than life, Plato laid the way for all the various ideologies that have denigrated physical existence—from negative existentialist philosophers who say that life is pointless, to fire-and-brimstone preachers who see earthly existence as purely evil. Aristotle was a corrective to this. By calling attention to the wonders of the physical world and mapping them with a clear eye to the order that they manifested, he created a tradition of disciplined observation and keen appreciation for the material world that played a huge part in shaping the spirit of modern science.

What we need today is a combination of the best of the Platonic and the Aristotelian spirit. That's the new vision that people are starving for, and that they are beginning to adopt because of what they are learning from personal experiences of their own. The Plato-Aristotle distinction has been recognized by many to lie at the very roots of who we are. (Arthur Herman, in his recent book *The Cave and the Light*, tells the entire story of Western culture using this basic difference between Plato and Aristotle as a framework.) It's vital that this knowledge not be confined to dusty old history books. It's knowledge we need now.

I believe the coming era will contain dire challenges, as everyone is beginning to realize, but it may also be one in which heaven and all it contains can be taken seriously again. If this happens—if enough people come forward and start talking about the kinds of experiences described in this book—the tide of belief will truly change. The Platonic and the Aristotelian spirits will come together as they never have before, and the biggest shift in worldviews in history will occur.

This isn't to say that, when this happens, the secrets of the incomprehensibly vast worlds of spirit that lie beyond the physical world will be put under a microscope and examined. The universe—and in particular that most mysterious, personal, and hard-to-define part of the universe called consciousness—simply can't be treated this way. To study consciousness, to study the things of heaven (the nonmaterial realms), you have to knock humbly and hopefully at the door, as Jesus suggested, and ask, not demand, to be let in. In that sense, you might say that science will have to become, once again, a kind of modern mystery religion. It will have to approach the truth humbly, hat in hand. It will have to relearn how to request things from the universe, rather than demanding them. In other words, it will have to submit to the evidence that the universe presents about itself. And the fact is that the universe has been presenting modern science with evidence that the universe is spiritual first, and physical second, for more than a hundred years. The problem isn't evidence, but the fact that so many scientists are too stubborn to look at it.

Science—and perhaps especially medicine—has always had an initiatory aspect. It has always been a club, with rules of membership and arcane language not understood by people on the outside, and ordeals and tests to pass before one can enter the inner sanctum and truly call oneself a member. I should know. I vividly remember the day I graduated from medical school, the day I performed my first solo operation, the day I was first instrumental in saving someone's life. Modern life is full of all kinds of groups with an initiatory aspect to them. College social and sports clubs . . . all of these organizations trace their initiation ceremonies (and the harrowing and sometimes controversial ordeals that still often accompany them) back to the rites of initiation that defined and shaped people's lives in so much of the ancient and primordial worlds. My whole skydiving career in college was nothing if not yet another—truly wonderful—initiatory club. I will never forget the three words my instructor—we might say my initiator—said to me that day back in September 1972 as the single-engine Cessna 195 we were in banked and straightened, and the door opened for my very first jump:

"Are you ready?"

Dear Dr. Alexander,

I am a Yoga and Spiritual teacher and so as my father was on his deathbed I saw that my mother was in great suffering. He was releasing his rage onto her as he lost control of his life. She continued to love him without conditions, yet felt bereft. Her life had twined around him. She even said to me that once he was gone, she would stop eating.

For three months prior to this I had asked Holy Spirit for two things. One, that my father would "feel" love. As a hard-driving, hard-living man he had always looked for happiness in the next raise, the next promotion, the next golf game. Angry and frustrated, I asked that he know this love throughout his being. Secondly, I asked that my mother would know, somehow, that he was alive even after he left his body.

. . . One day . . . He grabbed my mother's hand and mine and the tears rolled down his face. Looking at her he said, "I have looked all my life for you. You are the love of my life." He went on to say how much he loved my sister and me, and how much

we meant to him. Soon we were all crying and speaking from our heart. He went to sleep. When he awoke he had no memory of this. Yet, it had lifted my mother and me and I thanked the Divine for days afterwards.

[After my father died,] My mother asked me to come back in three weeks and help her quit eating. . . . In two weeks she called to say she was coming up from Florida to Maine to have Christmas with us. She had some exciting news—which had to be told in person. Once at my sister's home she brought me to sit on her bed. I asked her what had changed her so. "It's hard to believe," she said, "but three nights ago I awoke and your father was sitting at the end of my bed." "Was it a dream, Mom?" I asked. "No. He was more real than you are. And he looked to be 45 years old. He looked at me with such love, such complete love, that I knew he was waiting for me." I was struck by the change in her; no longer suffering, she was in a place of peace.

After this she decided to get an operation for an aneurism. . . . [T]he nurses said that she never complained and seemed to have a light around her. I noticed it myself. With physical therapy she attempted to recover her physical strength. But the operation was not a success. Serene, she asked to be unhooked from the breathing machine and I sat with her as she let go. We had much time to talk and laugh together and truly get to know each other before she left.

She knew that she was Pure Spirit having a human experience and was eternal and loved. Thank you Divine ONE and all the teachers who are here to help us know our True Nature.

The Gift of Meaning

I've come to feel that the journey I narrated in *Proof of Heaven* was a kind of modern mystery initiation: one in which, just like a mystery initiate, I died to my old view of the world and was born into a new one. So many people are going through versions of what I went through, spiritual experiences that change who they are. It's almost as if we, as a culture, are undergoing a mass initiation together. This is what the contemporary historian of ideas Richard Tarnas has suggested:

> *I believe humankind has entered into the most critical stages of a death-rebirth mystery. The entire path of Western civilization has taken humankind and the planet on a trajectory of initiatory transformation, first with the nuclear crisis, followed by the ecological crisis—an encounter with mortality that is no longer individual and personal but rather transpersonal, collective, planetary.**

This is not something that lies in the future. It's happening now. A new view of reality is slowly but surely building: not just within the minds of contemporary thinkers like Tarnas, but ordinary people. People who have caught a glimpse of who we really are, where we really came from, and where we are really going, and who are searching, like me, for a new vocabulary and worldview to fit it into.

This is not easily done. How do you replace your old vision of the world with a new one without falling into pure chaos?

---

*Tarnas, "Is the Psyche Undergoing a Rite of Passage?", from Singer, *The Vision Thing*, 262.

How do you take that step from one world of order to another one, without risking slipping and falling between the two? It requires courage. Courage that, I believe, if we ask for it, we will get.

It is the responsibility of scientists never to suppress knowledge, no matter how awkward that knowledge is, no matter how it may bother those in power. We are not smart enough to decide which pieces of knowledge are permissible and which are not.

—CARL SAGAN (1934–1996)

In her 1987 book *A Farther Shore* (recently republished as *Farther Shores*), physician Yvonne Kason writes of an NDE she underwent when, while traveling as a doctor-in-training with a sick patient, the small plane she was in went down in an icy Canadian lake. Yvonne struggled as the water flooded the cabin, trying to get her patient, strapped into a cumbersome gurney, through the front passenger door. By the time Kason realized the gurney was too wide to fit through, her hands were frozen and nearly useless. She crawled through the flooding doorway and paddled for shore.

Coughing violently, numb throughout her body, and barely keeping her face above the frigid water, Yvonne suddenly found herself floating, easily and tranquilly, several hundred feet above the lake. She could see herself, paddling for shore, and the semi-submerged plane she'd escaped from, with complete clarity. She knew the patient still strapped to the gurney in the plane was probably doomed, and that, given the speed of the current and the temperature of the water, she was as well. Yet she felt completely at peace. She knew that, whatever happened, she was deeply loved and taken care of. Nothing could go wrong.

Kason struggled to the frozen shore along with two others from the downed plane, and waited for rescue. A helicopter eventually arrived, and "floating between paranormal and normal consciousness," as she puts it in her book, Yvonne finally made it to a hospital, where nurses took her to a hydrotherapy room and immersed her in a whirlpool:

"As I was submerged in the hot, swirling water," she writes, "I felt my consciousness shrinking from its expanded state and pulled through the top of my head back down into my body. The sensation was similar to what I imagine a genie might feel when it is forcibly sucked back into its tiny bottle. I heard a whoosh, felt a downward pulling sensation, and was suddenly aware of being totally back in my body again."

It's an incredible story, but even more extraordinary is what happened to Kason in its wake. "The months of transformation that occurred after my Near Death Experience," she writes, "left me feeling psychologically strong, clear, and centered. I felt tremendous inner strength and the courage to speak honestly. The experience still remains a source of tremendous inspiration some 15 years later. More important, it began a process of spiritual transformation that has continued to this day."

But that transformation didn't happen all at once, or without some shocks to Kason's old view of reality. She writes:

> *When I finally returned to work, I had regained much of the feeling in my fingertips and I felt physically and emotionally well—but I still didn't know I had had a Near Death Experience, and I certainly didn't know an NDE could leave one's mind open to psychic input. Imagine my shock when, about two months after the plane wreck, I had my first psychic experience.*
>
> *After work one evening, I was driving to visit my friend Susan. As I stopped at a red light, a vivid, bright, and almost glowing image popped into my mind's eye: a brain coated in pus. The image was so clear I was stunned.*
>
> *I was certain the image I saw represented meningitis—an infection of the surface lining of the brain. I was also sure that it was Susan's brain. Initially, bewildered by the experience, I decided not to mention it to anyone. But, when I arrived at Susan's house, I asked her how she was feeling. She told me she had been suffering from a severe, unusual headache—a classic symptom of meningitis—for several hours. I didn't want to alarm her, but just to make sure, I asked her about other common symptoms of meningitis. Even though she didn't have any of them, the image of the horrible pus-covered brain haunted me, and I felt I had to say something. Hesitantly, I told her about the vision and what I thought it represented. She thought for a moment and then asked how she could tell if her headache did indicate early meningitis.*

Yvonne explained the symptoms and made Susan promise that if these developed, she would go to the emergency room. They did, and she did. "When she went to emergency," writes Yvonne, "the doctors did a spinal tap and confirmed that she had a rare, often-fatal type of meningitis. The early diagnosis allowed the doctors to treat her successfully, and she was able to return home in two weeks."

Yvonne at first didn't know what to do with this new capacity. It was only when she met my associate in near-death studies Kenneth Ring a few years later that she learned that a more awakened perception of the world is a common effect of near-death experiences.

Joseph Campbell, in his classic 1949 book, *The Hero with a Thousand Faces*, argued that all myths and legends are in essence one story. In a nutshell, that story runs like this: An individual going about his or her business (we'll call him a "him" for economy, though heroines of this nature are in no short supply) suddenly gets pulled out of that life and taken into a strange new landscape. There this individual suffers trials and traumas, which climax in a meeting with a god or goddess. If the hero is a man, the encounter usually takes the shape of a meeting with an extraordinarily beautiful and wise female being—an angel of sorts—who guides the hero to even higher realms; perhaps all the way to the Divine.

This angelic being is both totally different from the hero, yet at the same time—in that strange logic that myths and dreams can have—his deepest self.

Another common element of this universal story is that the

hero suffers from a wound of some kind: he has a weakness that tries and torments him, and keeps him from fulfilling his destiny. That meeting in the world beyond heals this wound. When the hero returns to the world he came from, he is a changed person. He has been initiated, and like all initiates he is now a citizen of two worlds.

There is often a segment in this story in which, once back, the hero wrestles with the significance of what happened to him. It certainly was real enough while it was happening. But was it all, perhaps, just a dream?

Then, through some small, perhaps seemingly insignificant event, his adventure and the lessons he learned in the world above are confirmed. He gets evidence, proof, that his adventure was real. He realizes, once and for all, that the place he went was no mere dream, and the treasure he brought back from it is solid and real as well.

Sound familiar?

Initiate/heroes are also often buried in crypts, tombs, or other such structures, where their bodies stay while their souls journey to other worlds. In my story, the "crypt" was Medical Intensive Care Unit bed 10, where I lay, immobile, surrounded by my friends and family while my real self journeyed to the Gateway and the Core. Shamans often have their family and friends gathered around them when they go into trances— when their soul leaves its body to travel in the worlds above and beneath the earth. So, too, I had my sons, Bond and Eben; my former wife, Holley; my mother, Betty; and my sisters Jean, Betsy, and Phyllis gathered around me, keeping a constant vigil until my journey was done.

My wound, meanwhile, was a lifelong subconscious struggle with feeling unworthy of being loved, resulting from my abandonment and adoption as an infant. In my NDE, my guardian angel gave me the supreme unconditional love that so many other out-of-body journeyers have come to know so well. Thus began my profound healing.

My story was particularly dramatic. But since coming back I've learned that versions of this story happen to people all the time. That is exactly why Campbell gave his book the title he did. We are, he was pointing out, all heroes. And we all undergo similar journeys. That's a big reason, I now realize, why I never tire of traveling around telling my story (something I've been doing practically nonstop since *Proof of Heaven* came out) and why people don't tire of hearing it. The more I tell it, the more strength it gives me; and the more I see it resonate in the eyes of those I tell it to, the greater my joy and gratitude.

Many initiatory scenarios involve the person facing and overcoming a devouring monster. Bacterial meningitis, the illness that I suffered from, and the illness that alerted Yvonne to her new psychic capabilities, was the modern medical equivalent of one of those fiery dragons or man-eating monsters that the initiatory heroes of myth and legend so often faced. Bacterial meningitis literally does try to eat you. Yvonne's ordeal in the freezing lake waters also reminded me that many initiatory scenarios begin with an immersion in water. My own story had, in fact, begun with an immersion as well—though of a very different sort. *Proof of Heaven* began with me getting out of bed early on a Monday morning with agonizing back pain, and stepping into my bathtub in an attempt to make the pain go away.

Water is a primary symbol of rebirth. The ancient mystery rituals often included immersion in water. The word *baptism* comes from the Greek *baptismos*, which means a ceremonial dip or washing. Baptism was and is a ceremonial way of washing away the "dirt" that has accrued on our earthly journey, so that we can recover our original, heavenly nature. Not that I was thinking about it like this at the time. At the time, I had horrific back pain, was edging up on being late for work, and just wanted to get on with my day.

Once I'd made it out of the tub, I put on my red terry-cloth bathrobe (red robes, a reader later informed me, had ritual significance in early Christian baptism ceremonies) and took what I describe as "baby steps" back to bed. As we went back and forth on this stretch of text, Ptolemy Tompkins, my collaborator on this book and on *Proof of Heaven*, kept taking "baby steps" out. I kept putting it back in. Later, Ptolemy said that I had been exactly right to leave the word in. Like many an initiate before me, I had first to become "like a little child" before I could travel back to my homeland. And on some level I knew this—even though consciously I didn't at all.

Here, as in so many other places in the story, the mythic-ritual details were simply . . . *there.* I was not planning on any of this symbolism ahead of time. Here in my story, just as everywhere in our lives, meaning is endemic to life. If we look for it, we will find it. We don't need to place it there.

The Gift of Meaning

Dear Dr. Alexander,

On Nov. 10, 2007, I was bitten by a venomous snake in La Grange, Texas. I received 6 units of blood and 18 units of antivenin after a 70-mile helicopter ride, and the ER in Austin was convinced that I would not survive. I was in the ICU for only two days, but for the first 12 hours or so I was unconscious. Although I don't remember the details like you did, I am convinced that I communicated with my father, who was in his final stages of Alzheimer's at the time. He passed not two months later, but two days before he passed, when I was visiting him, something very eye-opening happened. As we were getting ready to leave, the man who had been very much unresponsive and unrecognizing for months grabbed me by my hands with . . . his eyes wide open, [and] looked at me as if to say "It will be okay, go on now."

I never really told anybody about the event, even after he passed, other than my wife, who was with me at the time. I always felt that somehow we had communicated unknowingly, and now after reading your book, I am convinced that we did. Also, after my experience, I have changed the way that I feel about death (my own anyway), as in, there is no fear of dying and I almost feel invincible. Not in a suicidal way, but in a comfortable way, meaning I am not afraid of it, but almost embrace it. I have always believed in God, as has my family, but I feel that I have been in touch with God in a way that I still don't understand. I just want you to know that although I still don't understand completely what really happened to me during

my time of unconsciousness, I feel more and more that it wasn't
a dream. Thank you for your wonderful book and I wish you
continued success in getting the message out to as many people as
possible.

Thomas Mueller

The Dogon people of Africa have an interesting word for *symbol*: "word of this lower world." This material world is symbolic through and through. It is always trying to talk to us, trying to remind us of what lies behind and above it. When we read books or see movies, we expect symbolic undertones. But life itself is symbolic. Meaning is not something added onto life by us. It's there already.

This is why I've become increasingly interested in what the psychologist Carl Jung called synchronicity: the curious way that events in our seemingly random, meaningless world have of acting, on occasion, distinctly *un*random. We all experience synchronicities. Not just coincidences, but full-on conjunctions of events that practically *scream* meaning. Jung felt these events were so clearly real that they demanded scientific attention. It was a remarkable insight, given the heavily materialist mid-twentieth-century years in which he did most of his work.

And it was completely scandalous. "Meaning," to his fellow scientists, was not just an unscientific word—it was outright antiscientific. Science says that meaning is an illusion, a projection. We cook meaning up in our heads and then throw it onto the world, hoping it will stick. To embrace meaning as real would mean to plummet us back into the bottomless pit of ignorance and superstition that scientists spent such a long and laborious time dragging us out of. Philosophers and poets can ask what things mean. Scientists, Jung well knew, could not. Yet he went ahead and did so anyhow.

The most famous synchronicity in Jung's life occurred during a session with a patient of his who was describing a dream she'd had of being given a golden scarab: a carved Egyptian beetle.

"While she was telling me this dream," Jung writes, "I sat with my back to the closed window. Suddenly I heard a noise behind me, like a gentle tapping. I turned round and saw a flying insect knocking against the windowpane from outside. I opened the window and caught the creature in the air as it flew in."[*]

Keen observer of the natural world that he was, Jung quickly identified the beetle. "It was the nearest analogy to a golden scarab that one finds in our latitudes, a scarabaeid beetle, the common rose-chafer (*Cetonia aurata*), which contrary to its usual habits had evidently felt an urge to get into a dark room at this particular moment."[†]

All over the world today, people are undergoing experiences, from the vast to the seemingly trifling, that deliver a single message: the world has meaning. The higher worlds speak to us wherever we are. All we need to do is listen. Like

---

[*] Jung, *Synchronicity*, 31.
[†] Ibid.

me, these new initiates have had their eyes opened to a mystery that transcends all arguments between one religion and another, between religion and science, between belief and unbelief. We have become people for whom a damaging split deep within our psyches (one that we often didn't even know we had) has been healed. The spirit of Plato and the spirit of Aristotle are coming together in us. As a result, we have found ourselves living in a new world.

Dear Dr. Alexander,

Let me begin by telling you I have NEVER written an author before. On October 21, 2013, our 25-year-old son entered the hospital with what we thought was a case of stomach flu or food poisoning. He quickly got worse and was put in the ICU. We watched as he lost most of the functions of his organs, one after the other. His liver quit processing the antibiotics . . . his kidney function slowed way down . . . and then his pancreas wasn't working correctly. He had congestive heart failure, so his lungs were filling. Last his heart went into a-fib. They couldn't give him glucose in his IV because they were worried about sending him into a diabetic coma. He was hooked to 11 different IV bags. He wasn't responding well to any of it. We thought he was sleeping a lot. They never said he was in a coma, although his wrists and ankles "hooked" inward, as you explained in your book.

The hospital called in the chaplain, the pain specialist, [and] the palliative care specialist, gave us funeral brochures, and told us there was nothing more they could do. They said that, as each IV emptied, they were not going to replace it. We watched and prayed as they removed one after the other of the IV bags, down to the saline solution. As each bag was removed, his body began resuming the function of that organ . . . The MDs were just shaking their heads; one of them told me it was more than just what they did. We also had taken turns and never left him alone the 9 days in ICU or the other 20 days in the hospital. My son was moved to a regular room and then to the rehab center of the hospital. On November 4 his heart went into sinus rhythm on its own.

He was charming and bright. . . . His birthday was during his stay in rehab. One of the nurses brought him a new copy of your book Proof of Heaven. A couple of days later, during a quiet moment, I asked him if he wanted me to read a chapter. He said sure. After I was reading for a while, I looked over at him and my tough 6'4" man-son had tears streaming down his cheeks. I asked if the book was upsetting him and should I stop? He said no, to keep reading. He wanted me to continue for a couple more chapters.

That night as he was preparing to sleep, he quietly said, "I talked to God in ICU. He asked me if I wanted to stay or come home. I told Him I wanted to go home. I didn't know other people thought they went to heaven. We were beside Heaven's gates. There was lots of green beyond. I'll tell you more about it later."

Interestingly, a couple of days later, I asked the nurse when she read the book. She replied that she never had. She said

33

*someone recommended that she get the book for us, so she special
ordered it.*

*My son came home from the hospital on November 19, 2013.
Your book helped him come to grips with what had happened. . . .*

*We continued reading chapters until we reached the part
where you went home, too. Then he said we'd finish it later—in
a couple of weeks. He wanted to process it. We never finished it
together. We had him only six weeks at home; he never did tell us
more about his experience. He passed away on January 4, 2014
of H1N1: 2009 (swine) flu virus.*

*Thank you so much for writing your book. It helped us all
immensely. When my son passed away, I figure he went back to
Heaven's gates and talked to God again.*

Sincerely,
Claire

In December 1991, a well-known San Francisco psycho-analyst named Elizabeth Lloyd Mayer had a problem. Her daughter's irreplaceable harp was stolen at a concert. Mayer spent two months using every tool at her command to recover the harp. Finally, she writes in her book *Extraordinary Knowing*, a friend told her that if she was really ready to try anything to get the harp back, she should try a dowser. "The only thing I knew about dowsers," writes Mayer, "were that they were that strange breed who locate underground water with forked sticks." For Mayer, a professor of psychology at the University of California, Berkeley, this was unknown territory.

Mayer knew the notion that a lost possession of hers could

be located psychically by a perfect stranger was pure fantasy. It violated all the logical rules of the world in which she had been living and successfully practicing her craft as a psychiatrist for decades.

At the same time, she really wanted that harp back.

Doing her best to keep her inner critic at bay, Mayer dialed the number her friend had given her for a prominent dowser in Arkansas.

"Give me a second," said the dowser. "I'll tell you if it's still in Oakland." Yes, he said, it was. Using a street map, he indicated the exact house where, he said, the harp was located. Mayer wondered what to do with this information. She couldn't just knock on the door of the house with the news that a dowser had told her that her daughter's harp was there.

Then she had an inspiration. She printed some flyers about the harp and tacked them up in a two-block radius around the house.

Three days later, she got a phone call. The person on the other end of the line said they had seen the flyer, and that his neighbor had the harp. After some phone calls, a meeting was set up, and the harp was returned.

Driving home with her daughter's recovered harp in the backseat, Mayer had a three-word realization:

"This changes everything."

This story describes how a lot of us in the scientific community ended up changing our perspective on what kind of place the world is. We found ourselves in a situation where we were forced to try all the old explanations for some new piece of phenomena. When they didn't work, we were forced to consider the possibility that the world as we understood it was not the world as it actually is. This in turn led to our exploring new ways of understanding the world—ways that delivered better answers than our old methods did.

We may have known that these ways of looking at the world existed before, but thought them silly. We might *still* have thought them silly.

But . . . we wanted our harp back.

And so we took the risk. We gathered our courage and opened ourselves to the possibility of a new, and radically different, set of ideas about what kind of place the world might really be.

In the case of people like Dr. Mayer, the payoff we got from this was much bigger, much more important, than any harp. We recovered *ourselves*. We learned that, when it came to those three big questions that the cultures that came before us asked, there might really be some altogether different answers than we had ever dreamed there were.

Mayer's story also shows that you do not need to have a dramatic experience like an NDE to undergo this change in perspective. But I do believe that it is the duty of those of us who *have* undergone these more dramatic kinds of experiences to spread the word—to talk about where we've been and what we've seen, and to use every skill at our disposal to bring that message to life and to translate it back to this world.

Like me, Kason and Mayer were both doctors, and they were both dragged, kicking and screaming, into this new world where meaning is real. Both made it. They became doctors—high initiates in the club of science—who were not afraid to understand that meaning, the language of the spiritual world, is real. That another world is trying to talk to us, and that the more we listen, the more we will understand. The twin streams of science and spirit, rather than fighting, are entwined within these fellow physicians, rather like the way the two serpents of the caduceus entwine on the sacred staff that can be seen to this day in just about every doctor's office.

Dear Doctor Alexander,

My wife Lorraine passed away June 24, 2013 after 21 years of marriage. Throughout Lorraine's life she was very spiritual and as a member of the Arlington Metaphysical Church in Virginia practiced Reiki healing. Lorraine also had Native American "guides" that she turned to during challenging times. After Lorraine passed and I was confronted with the challenge of packing up my household in anticipation of moving off to my next abode, I would sit out on my deck trying to relax, and lo and behold a monarch butterfly appeared and flew around not more than 10 feet [from] where I was sitting. It seemed odd since there were no other butterflies to be seen. Having lived on my property for more than 14 years, I knew butterflies usually showed up in groups. However this particular butterfly had no companions. Also when I would need to go out, when I opened my garage door, the same butterfly would appear. I wasn't sure what to think. However, I made sure when I backed the car out that the butterfly did not end up as "road kill."

. . . I thought maybe Lorraine came back to earth as a butterfly but I needed more convincing. . . . I was skeptical about anything bordering on spirituality. . . . This is now the beginning of my quest for faith and peace of mind.

At the time of Lorraine's passing, I decided to donate her body to an organization that used the deceased for medical research. At the end of a set time period, Lorraine was to be cremated and her remains returned to me. Lorraine's final wish was to be buried next to a tree so her spirit would have access to her "guides." I'll get back to this in due course.

In the process of getting things packed in anticipation of my move, I had to go through Lorraine's personal items including all of her jewelry and miscellaneous items. As I opened her drawers in her jewelry box, I kept coming across items that depicted butterflies. I knew Lorraine liked butterflies, but she also liked other collectibles like gnomes, Dickens Village buildings and characters, ceramic cows, and best of all about 100 dolls that she collected and displayed throughout the house. Keep in mind while all of this packing was taking place, the monarch butterfly was always waiting for me to come outside.

. . . After getting situated in my townhouse, I had Lorraine's remains sent to me. I opened the shipping box and took out a 4" x 6" box with a nice cord tied around it in a bow. It had hardly any weight and ironically a song came into my mind as I picked up the box containing Lorraine's ashes: it was Peggy Lee singing "Is that all there is?" I put Lorraine up on my bookcase in my

*office and contemplated as to how to fulfill her final wish. After
2 weeks of holding on to what was left of Lorraine, I came up
with a plan. I would ask my friend Norman if it was ok to find
a final resting place for Lorraine on his daughter's 13 acres of
forest on the side of South Mountain in Maryland. . . . So one
day I arranged with Norman to bring Lorraine to this little
piece of heaven and find a good solid tree where Lorraine could
rest in peace.*

    *As we got onto the property and started to discuss where we
could find the "right" tree, lo and behold a monarch butterfly
appeared and flew around near where we were standing. As
before when I saw the butterfly on the deck of my old house . . .
only one butterfly appeared. . . . After locating the right
spot, Norman helped dig a deep enough hole to accommodate
Lorraine's ashes. I now undid the cord around the box and
opened it up. Inside was a plastic bag containing what was left
of my beloved wife and soul mate. I then untied the plastic bag
and committed Lorraine to her final resting place. During all
this time, the monarch butterfly remained in the same area where
we left it. I now had a strong feeling that Lorraine was there in
the form of that monarch butterfly.*

    *To reinforce my belief, here comes the icing on the cake.
Yesterday I called Norman and told him I would like to come out
to the cabin to see him and meet his daughter for the first time.
Yesterday was about 10 days after we buried Lorraine. When
I got there and we were walking around the property, guess
who was flying around all by herself. Yup! You guessed right. It
was the same monarch butterfly that came into my life around*

a month ago. After reading my story you can choose to believe or disbelieve. You can say that monarch butterflies are common throughout the area but keep in mind this was always one butterfly alone.

Don Entlich

If your husband died, and he loved cardinals, and on the anniversary of his death you happen to walk out to his memorial and you find a cardinal sitting on it, you are allowed to take this as a sign. Don't let some voice inside you tell you that the cardinal's presence there is a coincidence. Not unless you understand the word *coincidence*, which means two things occupying one place, in terms of the deeper and better term, *synchronicity*.

"If you smile at me," a line from a Crosby, Stills and Nash song popular in my college days runs, "I will understand, because that is something everybody everywhere does in the same language." The universe speaks one language, and it is the language of meaning. Meaning is built into every level of the universe—even the level we live on, where it's hardest to see. That's why the chief complaint that people have about modern life is that it's meaningless. Under the surface, it is anything but.

CHAPTER 3

The Gift of Vision

Where there is no vision the people perish.
—PROVERBS 29:18

Plato didn't use the word, but I suspect he would have appreciated our modern English term *murky* to describe our situation. The word comes from *myrk*, an old English word meaning "darkness." But there's also a strong sense, when we hear it, of earth, of muddiness. And that makes sense, because the darkness we struggle with while here on earth is precisely *that* kind of darkness. St. Paul presents the best-known version of this idea when, in First Corinthians, he talks about us seeing our world "as through a glass darkly." Earth, traditional wisdom suggests, is a place where it's hard to see.

But the vision that earthly life obscures so radically is not physical vision. It's spiritual vision: the vision that allows us to see where we are in the spiritual universe, just as physical vision allows us to see where we are in the physical world.

Two hundred years ago, when the modern scientific worldview was still in its youth, the poet William Blake came up with a name for the refusal on the part of the scientific community to see and acknowledge the spiritual side of the world. He called that refusal, and the philosophy that arose with it, Single Vision.

Now I a two-fold vision see . . .
May God us keep
From single vision, and Newton's sleep.

The "Newton" Blake mentions here is Sir Isaac Newton: mathematician, physicist, and formulator of the law of gravitation. Newton is one of the greatest scientists in history—perhaps even *the* greatest. But along with all his achievements, he was also guilty of a mistake. In line with this passage by René Descartes, he divided the world into an "inside" and an "outside," and said that only the latter was truly real:

I observed that nothing at all belonged to the nature of essence of body except that it was a thing with length and breadth and depth, admitting of various shapes and various motions. I found also that its shapes and motions were only modes, which no power could make to exist apart from it; and on the other hand that colors, odors, savours and the rest of such things, were merely sensations existing in my thought and differing no less from bodies than pain differs from the shape and motion of the instrument which inflicts it.

42

Once science had measured everything in the "outside" material world, Newton and other scientists of his day believed, they would know all there was to know. They left consciousness out of the picture. Why include it? You couldn't find it. You couldn't hunt it down and measure it. You couldn't weigh it. So that must have meant it wasn't real.

Our world is still built on that old distinction between matter (the world "out there") and mind (the world "in here") that Descartes established. "For better or worse," writes the psychologist Lawrence LeShan in his 2013 book, *A New Science of the Paranormal*, "this is a scientific culture. We listen to religious leaders, gurus, and politicians, but the people we believe speak real truth are the scientists."

LeShan then asks what might happen if—as I believe is inevitable—science begins to take the spiritual world seriously:

> *Shortly, it would be common knowledge—of the sort we mean when we use the phrase "everybody knows"—that there was more to the human being than is shown by the senses and that we are not permanently stuck inside our own skins. But these facts have not really touched us. They do not pose a threat to the everyday world of our senses. The walls of our lives do not come tumbling down. I go on as I was before, after I learn that the apparently solid desk I lean on is just an empty space with areas of mass, charge, and velocity racing around in it—that it is composed of, in Werner Heisenberg's phrase, "empty space haunted by singularities."**

---

*LeShan, *A New Science of the Paranormal*, 81–82.

We will wake up from Newton's sleep.

Dear Dr. Alexander,

On August 19, 1999, my dad had been in our local hospital's hospice unit for 13 days. He had had a series of strokes that left him in an unresponsive state. After much discussion with his doctors, it was the family's decision to "let him go."

My three siblings and I were at his bedside 24/7 those last few days. Someone was always in the room with him. At around 4:00 AM, he started that particular breathing pattern that lets you know the end is coming. We had been expecting it sooner, but dad was tough and in no rush to go.

The room was pitch dark except for a single night-light that was built into the wall and lighted a small floor area. We were on the 6th or 7th floor so no streetlights were shining in the room's windows.

Dad took his last breath. His feet and hands were already cool. I was sitting about a foot away from the bed, my head resting in the palm of my hands, my elbow on my knee. He was turned towards me, his head not more than a foot away from mine. As I was about to get up and stretch and talk to my brother and sisters, something caught my eye. It looked like a piece of dust had settled on dad's temple. Then I thought, how can I see this "dust"? The room is almost black yet I can see this! How is it illuminated? I looked around for some source of light that could be shining on dad's head—but there was none.

I closed my eyes to rest them for a moment, rubbed them with

44

my fingers, and opened them—and the dust was still there, still somehow visible. I inched closer, thinking it would have to float away. But it didn't. Then, as I watched, something started to extricate itself from the side of my dad's head! My eyes were wide open and I was breathing very slowly, trying to understand what I was seeing. . . .

A small orb, no larger than a quarter inch, very slowly surfaced from under my dad's temple. It was the color of that beautiful intense blue you find at the base of a candle flame. It was radiating white rays. They reminded me of 4th of July sparklers, but the sparks were radiating in slow motion. After maybe a minute, the entire orb had emerged and appeared to be resting on dad's temple. A tiny blue globe radiating white sparking rays.

After a few seconds, the orb slowly levitated to maybe two feet above dad's body and hovered there for a few seconds. Then it slowly drifted higher and toward the west side of the room (actually, more than drifted—it seemed to want to go in a particular direction), and then rose and went into the ceiling and was gone.

I was still sitting in my chair, turned to be looking to where the orb departed. I turned around, expecting someone to say something—but nobody did. I didn't want to ask any questions that would have me putting words in my siblings' mouths, so I simply asked, "Did something just happen?"

My sister said: "You mean that light that just came out of the side of dad's head?"

I think Shakespeare was right when he said, "There are

more things in heaven and earth than are dreamt of in your
philosophy."

David Palmer, Higganum, CT

"Did something just happen?"
"Did you see that?"
"Did you feel what I just felt?"
People ask each other questions like this all the time in situations like David's: situations in which a loved one is passing, and something inexplicable—something more than simply physical—accompanies the event. The scientific method demands that a phenomenon be visible to more than one person. It also demands that the phenomenon be repeatable. That's where stories like David's—and they are incredibly common—become easy prey for the critics.

Or so most people think.

During my graduate years at Duke University Medical Center in Durham, North Carolina, I would often pass an unassuming little building near campus called the Institute of Parapsychology (now named Rhine Research Center). I never gave it much thought. No doubt all kinds of well-meaning folk were hard at work inside, making test subjects guess what random cards were being drawn from a deck, and things of that nature.

Such experiments were indeed going on within the walls of the Rhine Center. What I didn't know was that those experiments, and others like them, conducted in small but reputable institutions set up inside universities in the United States,

Canada, the United Kingdom, and elsewhere, have established beyond the slenderest statistical probability that telepathy, precognition, and similar phenomena of non-local consciousness are real.

But what has become of this discovery? As LeShan points out, precious little. The problem is not whether phenomena beyond the ability of materialistic science to explain exist. They do. The problem is getting this news into our bones. Into our blood. The problem is turning ourselves into something different than we were before.

The problem is actually *transforming*.

We have always known who we are. That knowledge has emerged, sunk out of sight, and resurfaced more times and in more places than anyone could count. It's as old as the Paleolithic (the Old Stone Age, some thirty thousand years ago), when our forebears were already burying their loved ones in the fetal position, decked with flowers and shells, to suggest that though their bodies were buried in the earth, they would be reborn in a world beyond. And it is as recent as the 2014 experimental confirmation of physicist John Stewart Bell's 1964 theorem that paired particles separated by millions of light-years will move in instantaneous concert with each other, because time and distance are themselves illusions.

We have *always* lived in the real universe. That has never changed. We are the ones who have changed, again and again. We are the ones who have drifted away from that real universe, come back to it, and drifted away again. But we have never been quite so far away, for quite so long a time, as we are now. Everyone now knows the consequences of treating nature as an object—a dead thing we can manipulate to our liking. We know—physically speaking—that as a planet we are in deep trouble. But not everyone knows that the solution to this problem will have to be spiritual as well as material— that we have to change not only the way we live, but what we think about those three big questions that the people who came before us were smart enough to never let out of their sight. Why? Because the only way to live happily on the earth is in the light of heaven. To live without heaven is to be a slave to one's suppressed yearning for the completion that the knowledge of its existence provides. It's not hard to see how that suppressed yearning has led to so many of the excesses that have made our planet the profoundly damaged and en-dangered place that it is today.

Have you ever seen a fox in the wild? As a North Carolina native I've seen plenty, and they're always a beautiful sight. Picturing an animal like that is a great way to understand what was given to us by Newton, Galileo, Descartes, and the other architects of the new scientific vision of the world that was born in the sixteenth century, and what they took from us as well.

Imagine what a peasant in the Middle Ages saw when he or she looked at a fox. The animal itself was there, but so was a huge mass of biblical, mythological, and folkloric associa-tions that didn't necessarily belong with it. The fox was cun-ning, sensual, dishonest, sinful . . . all kinds of human things it blatantly *wasn't,* but that an individual of this time, trained in large part to see nature through the lens of the Bible, couldn't help but see it as.

When science came into its own in the sixteenth century, it made a revolutionary break with all those old associations. Foxes, the pioneers of the age of science discovered, aren't crafty, sensual, sinful beings. They're animals—canine members of the mammalian class, with a range of such and such territory, a gestation period of so many weeks. But they were no longer anthropomorphic sinful scoundrels.

Aristotle used logic to think about the world, but he did not use the scientific method. He didn't get out there and *test.* (As pointed out earlier, we have the alchemists to thank for coming up with the rudiments of the experimental aspect of the scientific method that modern science eventually adopted.) In the past, no one had bothered to dissect a fox, to compare its skull structure with those of other carnivores, to see how its heart or its liver or its intestines differed or didn't differ from those of a cow or a goose or a human being. The fathers of the Scientific Revolution took the Aristotelian spirit of direct observation a step further. They no longer just looked at the world and thought about it—they took it apart, down to its smallest piece.

In addition to being tremendously useful, this brave new way of looking at the world was also deeply honest. *Respect the reality of the physical world,* this approach tells us. *Don't get lost in some imagined dogmatic religious system that pastes its imagined meanings on the world and the things in it. Go out and investigate that world yourself, and find out what it really is.*

And all that is wonderful. But of course, we know what soon happened. We went too far. Along with the advances of modern science—of being able to study an animal like a fox and see it in a truly complex, sophisticated way—we also got the attitude that the world and everything in it was nothing more than an object to capture, kill, dissect, and most important, *use*. Before long, foxes—along with everything else in the world—became seen for their material value, and that alone. The fox became a predator of chickens and other useful livestock, the carrier of a pelt that was valuable as a garment, an animal useful in limited numbers as an object of sport . . . and not much else.

But a fox is much more than that. It is a multidimensional creature whose current form is physical but whose real nature is spiritual.

Just like us.

After death a man is nonetheless a man.*
—EMANUEL SWEDENBORG

Getting back that multidimensional view—that ability to see foxes, ourselves, and everything else on earth within the context of the spiritual universe—is the essence of the new

---

*TCR 792, quoted in Van Dusen, *The Presence of Other Worlds,* 72.

vision, that marriage of science and spirit that is on its way at last. It's a view of the world that isn't "religious" in the old, ponderous, dogmatic sense of the word, or "scientific" in the reductive, materialistic, objectifying sense of the word, either. It's a way of seeing the world that is capable of taking its measure, of studying it scientifically, but without getting lost in the terrible one-dimensionality of the purely materialist view.

Even before our current moment there were scientists who understood that rationalism needed to be reborn if it was to be truly useful. The eighteenth-century writer Johann Wolfgang von Goethe, a great poet and also one of the fathers of modern science, probably had the ancient mystery religions in mind when he wrote these famous lines:

> . . . *so long as you haven't experienced this: to die and so to grow, you are only a troubled guest on the dark earth.**

Even today in the modern scientific world, Goethe suggests in these lines, we must be initiates. Without initiation into knowledge of our true identities and the place we really came from, we lose our bearings. For those blinded by this lack of knowledge, the world becomes a very dark place indeed.

When the great scientist and mathematician Blaise Pascal died in 1662, this note was found sewn in his jacket:

---

*From "The Holy Longing" by Johann Wolfgang von Goethe, translated from the German by Robert Bly.

The year of grace 1654

Monday, 23 November, feast of Saint Clement, Pope and Martyr, and of others in the Martyrology.

Eve of Saint Chrysostomus, Martyr and others.

From about half past ten in the evening to about half an hour after midnight.

Fire.

God of Abraham, God of Isaac, God of Jacob,

Not the God of philosophers and scholars.

Absolute certainty: Beyond reason. Joy. Peace.

Forgetfulness of the world and everything but God.

The world has not known thee, but I have known thee.

Joy! joy! joy! tears of joy! *

Gustav Fechner was a respected nineteenth-century physicist and one of the fathers of modern experimental psychology. In his book *The Religion of a Scientist*, he wrote the following:

One spring morning I went out early. The fields were greening, the birds were singing, the dew glistening. . . . There fell on everything a transfiguring light; it was only a tiny fraction of the earth, only a tiny moment of its existence and yet as I comprised more and more in the range of my vision, it seemed to me not only so beautiful but so true and so evident that it is an angel, so rich and fresh and blooming, and at the same time so stable and unified, moving in the heavens, turning wholly towards heaven its

---

*Pascal, the Fragment, quoted in Happold, *Mysticism*, 39.

animated face and bearing me with it to that same heaven—so
beautiful and so true that I wondered how men's notions could be
so perverted as to see in the earth only a dry clod, and to seek for
angels apart from earth and stars or above them in the vacant
*heaven, and never find them.**

Dr. Alexander,

I read your book (received as a gift from a very intuitive and
intelligent friend), with interest, as I had an inexplicable
experience about a quarter century ago, which I can recall to this
day. It was not an NDE as I was not sick or incapacitated in
any way. I was coming back from court (I am still practicing
law) heading toward my car. I specifically recall stepping
on a crack in the cement sidewalk and (without warning
nor explanation) I suddenly became completely aware that
everything was absolutely okay. When I say "everything,"
I mean everything in as expansive a term as anyone could
imagine—including (as lawyers like to say) without limiting
the generality of the foregoing, the past, present, future, the
universe, the cosmos, all actions, all events, all circumstances that
were, are or could ever be. When you talk about "ultra reality"
in your book, I can understand what you are talking about. The
feeling that everything in the universe was okay—exactly as
it should be—was more true, more real, more direct than any

---

*Fechner, *Religion of a Scientist: Selections from Gustav Fechner*, edited and translated by Walter Lowrie, 153, quoted in Anderson, *The Face of Glory*, 156.

experience I have ever had. Being a lawyer, I am trained (and naturally inclined anyway) to argue or debate anything, but this feeling transcended any possibility of argument, debate or doubt. Driving back to my office, the feeling disappeared after about five minutes—never to return.

Kenneth P.

Goethe, Pascal, and Fechner didn't possess the scientific knowledge we do today, but each was a member of the modern world, and each was, in his time, a scientific giant on whose shoulders we stand today. The same is true of the seventeenth-century scientist Emanuel Swedenborg. Swedenborg spent most of his life as inspector of mines for Sweden, a job requiring considerable knowledge of engineering, physics, and the practical application of the new hydraulic techniques for the deep extraction of coal and other minerals just then coming into use in Europe at that time. Swedenborg was also an accomplished geometer, chemist, and anatomist, and the first person to formulate a rough idea of what the cerebellum, the portion of the brain responsible in large part for motor coordination, actually does. He was, by any measure, a genius.

Swedenborg had a particular interest in the brain, and spent many years trying to isolate the seat of consciousness—the physical location of what, back in his time, was still called the soul. Then, in the middle of his life, Swedenborg discovered (as the psychologist and Swedenborg scholar Wilson Van Dusen put it) that he had been "looking in the wrong place." Swedenborg underwent a spiritual crisis. A series of terrifyingly vivid dreams finally led to a moment in which the heavens themselves seemed to open. Swedenborg's old world cracked, buckled, and collapsed. A new one grew up in its place.

Swedenborg devoted the rest of his life to studying and cataloguing the spiritual worlds he had discovered, with the same rigor that he had previously devoted to studying the physical world. Swedenborg was the first modern scientist to treat heaven as a real place, and the first to try to map it.

Cultivating a style of "inner observation" in which he would slip into a kind of meditative trance, Swedenborg catalogued a vast series of worlds, which he wrote about in copious detail. These writings are often quite outlandish, and got him into a lot of trouble with his fellow scientists, and with the gatekeepers of doctrinaire Christianity as well. The worlds Swedenborg explored had people and trees and houses in them. He spoke with angels and demons. He described, with the precision of a modern weatherman detailing a cold front, the spiritual climates of the different worlds he visited.

The specific character of each of these worlds was determined by one factor above others: the amount of love or hate present in them. If you were a person defined by love, Swedenborg said, you ended up in one of the innumerable spiritual zones that together made up what Swedenborg understood as heaven. If you were defined by hate, you ended up in hell.

Swedenborg was a believer in the ancient idea of the microcosm—that each of us is a kind of universe in miniature. If we look inside ourselves the right way, he said, we will not only find a map of heaven, we will find heaven itself. Our whole idea of what is "external" and therefore real, and "internal" and therefore imaginary, is based on our experiences here in the material domain, where consciousness is mediated by the brain and we move about in a physical body that we have become brainwashed into thinking is our total identity. The truth is that what we experience as our "inner" self isn't "inside" us at all, and when someone like Swedenborg says that there are whole worlds "within" us, he is not talking about our capacity to imagine unreal places. He is saying that the universe is a spiritual place more than a physical one, and that the spiritual universe has many worlds—"many mansions," as Jesus put it—and these worlds are truly that: *worlds*, with clouds and breezes and cities and climates and people. "The more a man surrenders to God," Swedenborg scholar Ursula Groll writes, "and unfolds this 'heaven' in himself, the nearer the human comes to God and the more he becomes a man, because he has a greater share in the cosmic consciousness or the all-embracing whole."* In other words, mapping heaven was, for Swedenborg, not only legitimate science; it was something we need to do in order to be truly human.

Heaven, wrote the Persian mystic Najmoddin Kobra, using language that is wonderful in its fearless directness, is not the "visible outer sky." There are, he said, "other skies, more profound, more subtle, bluer, purer, brighter, innumerable

---

* Groll, *Swedenborg and New Paradigm Science*, 78.

and limitless." Really other skies? Yes. Kobra means this. He is not speaking metaphorically. But these regions can only be entered by people who are spiritually attuned to them. In the universes beyond the physical, you cannot just march into new territories and conquer them. You have, instead, to tune yourself to them, to harmonize with them, or they will remain closed off. "The purer you become within," Kobra wrote, "the purer and more beautiful is the Sky that appears to you, until finally you are walking in divine purity. But divine purity is also limitless. So never believe that beyond what you have reached there is nothing more, nothing higher still."*

I know that mystics like Kobra, and mystic-scientists like Swedenborg, are right. Heaven isn't an abstraction; it isn't a dreamscape cooked up from empty, wishful thinking. It is a place as real as the room or the airplane or the beach or the library where you are right now. It has objects in it. Trees, fields, people, animals . . . even (if we are to listen to the Book of Revelation or the twelfth-century Persian visionary Suhrawardi or the twelfth-century Arabic philosopher and mystic Ibn 'Arabi) actual cities. But the rules of how things work there—the laws of heaven's physics, if you will—are different from ours. The one rule we need to remember from here, however, is that we end up, in the end, where we belong, and we are led by the amount of love we have in us, for love is the essence of heaven. It is what it is made of. It is the coin of the realm.

---

*Quoted in Corbin, *The Man of Light in Iranian Sufism*, 60.

We are wise to apply that principle in our earthly lives as well—to *truly* love ourselves as the divine, eternal spiritual beings that we are, and pass along that love to our fellow beings and to all of creation. By serving as conduits for the unconditional love of the Creator for the creation, by showing compassion and forgiveness, we bring healing energy of infinite capacity into all levels of this material realm.

That's also why the main quality required of us if we are to catch a glimpse of this zone while alive on earth is not great intellect, nor great bravery, nor great cunning, fine as all those qualities are. What it takes is honesty. Truth can be approached in a thousand different ways. But because, as Plato himself said, like attracts like, what we need in order to apprehend truth more than anything else is to be truthful ourselves, and honest about the goodness and waywardness at work inside us. On this, voices as disparate as Buddha's, Jesus', and Einstein's are unanimous. Like understands like. The universe is based on love, but if we have no love in ourselves, the universe will be shut off from us. We will spend our lives triumphantly declaring that the spiritual world doesn't exist because we have failed to awaken the love in ourselves that alone will render this most obvious of facts visible to us. You cannot come to truth dishonestly. You cannot come to it telling lies to yourself, or to others. You cannot come bringing only a superficial sliver of yourself, while your larger, deeper self is left behind. If you want to see all of heaven, you have to bring all of yourself, or else just stay home.

CHAPTER 4

The Gift of Strength

Once a tigress attacked a herd of goats. A hunter saw her from a distance and killed her. The tigress was pregnant and gave birth to a cub as she expired. The cub began to grow in the company of the goats. At first it was nursed by the she-goats, and later on, as it grew bigger, it began to eat grass and bleat like the goats. Gradually the cub became a big tiger; but still it ate grass and bleated. When attacked by other animals, it would run away, like the goats. One day a fierce-looking tiger attacked the herd. It was amazed to see a tiger in the herd eating grass and running away with the goats at its approach. It left the goats and caught hold of the grass-eating tiger, which began to bleat and tried to run away. But the fierce tiger dragged it to the water and said: "Now look at your face in the water. You see, you have the pot-face of a tiger; it is exactly like mine." Next it pressed a piece of meat into its mouth. At first the grass-eating tiger refused to eat the meat. Then it got the taste of the meat and relished it. At last the fierce tiger said to the grass-eater: "What a disgrace! You

lived with the goats and ate grass like them!" And the other was
*really ashamed of itself.**
—SRI RAMAKRISHNA, NINETEENTH-CENTURY HINDU SAGE

When I was a kid, I loved Superman—in particular, the
fifties black-and-white TV series featuring George
Reeves. Like a lot of kids with their favorite superheroes, I
didn't just admire Reeves's Superman. I identified with him.
At age six or seven, if I walked, kitchen-towel cape tucked
into the neck of my pajamas, into a room where my sisters
were busy with other matters and didn't take immediate notice
of me, I'd laugh to myself. Didn't they realize whom they had,
right there in their midst?

But it wasn't just Superman's strength, his ability to fly, or
his X-ray vision that appealed to me, though those were fine
things indeed. It was that Superman *came from somewhere else.*
Though he did a good enough job of fitting in with the rest
of ordinary humanity, Superman wasn't from earth. Like the
tiger in the Hindu sage Ramakrishna's story quoted above,
he lived in a world where he was supposed to believe he was
one kind of being, while all along, beneath the surface, he was
really someone else.

Of course, I wasn't the only kid in the world who loved
Superman. I had plenty of friends at school who were fans of
other superheroes, too. Spider-Man. Iron Man. The Hulk. Yet

---

*From *The Gospel of Sri Ramakrishna.*

as I look back (and as I note the resurgence of the popularity of these heroes with kids today), I realize that just about all these characters had similar core themes going on with them as well. These were characters that had a secret identity. The world thought they were one thing, but they were really something else.

"Man is a god in ruins," Ralph Waldo Emerson famously wrote in his essay "Nature," and while this sounds negative, he was really suggesting just what Ramakrishna is in the story that started this chapter: that we are something extremely large that has mistakenly come to believe that it is very small. When we relearn to reappraise ourselves this way, we get stronger. And I mean a lot stronger.

Psychologists at the end of the nineteenth century made a very interesting discovery: when we repress the truth, we suffer for it. If deep down we know something is true but we walk around pretending it isn't, it creates a conflict; and this conflict, in turn, prevents the different parts of ourselves from communicating with each other effectively. Parts of us get split off and ignored. And the more they're ignored, the angrier they get—the more frustrated. A man cannot serve two masters, Jesus said, and a house divided cannot stand. In saying this, Jesus made not only one of the greatest spiritual statements, but one of the greatest psychological ones as well.

"The believer," wrote the French sociologist Emile Durkheim (1858–1917), "is not merely a man who has seen new truths of which the unbeliever is ignorant; he is a man who is *stronger*. He feels within him more force, either to endure the trials of existence or to conquer them. It is as though he were raised above the miseries of the world, because he is raised above his condition as a mere man."*

Belief moves mountains. But today we are told that while belief is certainly useful from a pragmatic standpoint, in order to have such belief we must be naïve. We must suppress our realistic, Aristotelian side and drift off into our interior, dreamy, Platonic side. In short, we must fool ourselves. "Science" has rendered real optimism about who we are and where we're going impossible.

That's one reason why many readers with a scientific background were so taken aback by the title of *Proof of Heaven.* "You simply can't *prove* that kind of thing," they said.

Interestingly, many readers who came to the book from a religious point of reference agreed. Faith, they argued, and the subjects of faith (heaven, a loving God), are not experimental subjects to be proved. To take a spiritual matter and try to demonstrate it by methods suitable only to physical situations—to lower lofty spiritual matters to the status of a chemistry project—is hubristic in the extreme.

I agree. Spiritual matters can never be proved or disproved using the old-fashioned, aggressive style of science that originated in the sixteenth century. But what if we approach these matters using a different kind of scientific approach? One built not on grabbing but asking? An approach that a scientist like Pascal, Fechner, Goethe, or Swedenborg might have approved of?

I find it interesting that, just as with those scientists, if we

*Durkheim, *Elementary Forms of Religious Life*, quoted in Hardy, *The Spiritual Nature of Man*, 8.

look at the lives and teachings of many of the greatest spiritual teachers, knowledge and faith are never far apart. Faith, it turns out, is much more concerned with evidence than we often realize. The Epistle to the Hebrews, in the single most significant statement on faith in all of literature, says that faith is "the substance of things hoped for, the evidence of things unseen."

Substance. Evidence. These words have a curiously scientific ring to them. The fact is, science and faith, the two ways of knowing the world that have defined our culture, are much, much more entwined than we tend to think they are. The whole concept of "faith" on one side of the room and "science" on the other is a fantasy. Human knowledge doesn't proceed along such neat and tidy lines, no matter how many neat and tidy-minded people might want it to. "In order to know, you must first believe," St. Anselm of Canterbury wrote in the eleventh century. He was echoing St. Augustine, who, almost a millennium before, said: "Believe so that you may understand." Without an initial faith that there is an order to the world and that it is an order we can know, science can't find out a single thing about the true nature of the universe. Knowledge does indeed, as St. Anselm suggested, require belief—one based on the essential integrity of the order that we encounter "out there" in the universe and "in here," in ourselves. To understand the world, we have to believe that the world makes sense, and that it is open to being understood by us. That is the hidden faith component in all science.

That's one of the many interesting things about the very strange and very exciting time we are living in right now.

Advances in science—especially physics but also in areas like remote viewing, telepathy, and the super-physical ordering structures that biologists like Rupert Sheldrake have demonstrated are at work behind the growth and behavior of plant and animal organisms—not to mention the ever-increasing evidence of the reality of near-death experiences, are pushing science and the "things unseen" of which Paul spoke in Hebrews ever closer together.

At the bottom of all this is the growing understanding that however many ways there are to approach it, there is one truth, not many. And it's the truth of the old spiritual world that we used to be on such good terms with, before the arguments of dogmatic religion and dogmatic science arrived to obscure it.

The fact is, we *can* prove heaven exists. The spiritual world is real, and people encounter it every day. You probably have. And inside, you know that. But you have been told that what you experienced as real isn't really real at all. That's the negative legacy of geniuses like Newton and the other fathers of the Scientific Revolution. But the thing about science—real science—is that when something's off, when a theory is no longer holding up, science adjusts or abandons it. Whether materialist science likes it or not, that is what is now happening.

Dear Dr. Alexander,

In 1952, at the age of 8, I was diagnosed with a brain abscess. Surgery was performed and afterward I was in a coma for two weeks. During that time I believe I had a near death experience.

The Gift of Strength

*When I awoke my mother was at my side and I asked why she
looked worried. She explained how ill I had been and I told her
she didn't need to worry, I was with Aunt Julie. This great-aunt
had recently passed. I vividly remember sitting in her lap and
being comforted by her. Yes, it might have been a dream, but I
don't think so. This many years later it's still clear in my mind. I
made a full recovery and have had a good life. Your book, Proof of
Heaven, was so like my story. I had to share.*

Jane-Ann Rowley

Plato's master Socrates famously displayed this strength—
the strength that comes when we have really said yes to heaven
in the face of popular opinion—when he was sentenced to
death by poison for corrupting the youth of Athens. Next to
that of Jesus, the death of Socrates is the most significant in
Western history. Plato's description of the heroic—indeed,
superhuman—tranquility with which Socrates drank the
hemlock administered to him by his Athenian jailers ranks as
one of the most powerful scenes in world literature. To die like
that, Plato knew, was not something one could accomplish
simply by virtue of strength of character—though Socrates
certainly had that. Socrates's supreme nonchalance in the face
of death was the result of knowledge of what death really *was*:
not an ending but a return to our truest home.

At the heart of all spiritual belief lies the intuition that we
are not who we think we are. That we are not just beings made
of earth, destined to walk about for a time and then fade away.

It's this intuition—buried but always ready to be awakened—that the world's spiritual traditions (and specifically the initiatory components of those traditions) tirelessly seek to wake us up to. *You're right,* say the spiritual traditions through their rich retinue of myths and dramatic initiatory scenarios. *You are not who you think you are. You are something much, much larger. But in order to become that larger being, you will have to die to the simple earthly person you are now. You must become a heavenly one as well.* These traditions ask us what the jumpmaster of the first parachute jump I ever took asked me.

Are you ready?

CHAPTER 5

The Gift of Belonging

*I myself believe that the evidence for God
lies primarily in inner personal experiences.*

—WILLIAM JAMES

In the 1960s, a British marine biologist named Alister Hardy, who at that point was known chiefly for his work on the biology of the Gulf Stream, established a center to study the "inner" component of human beings. This component, Hardy felt, had not been successfully explained by brain science. He believed there was more to the mind than the brain, and he wanted to find out what, if anything, ordinary people might have to tell him about this.

Hardy and his team sent out a series of questionnaires, and collected more than three thousand accounts from people who had come in direct contact with this inner dimension. Hardy was open to hearing from anyone who had a legitimate story to tell, his only caveat being that he was interested in ordinary people who had had actual experiences—no sermons, no tracts, no attempts to convince Hardy or his associates of this or that dogmatic religious truth. Hardy was interested in data, not propaganda. He was a true scientist—a seeker of truth. He just chose to look for it in an area where most of his fellow scientists believed there was none to be found.

Hardy made no pretense that the work he was doing was scientific by laboratory standards. He knew that the accounts he would receive would contain nothing you could isolate in a beaker or measure on a scale. But that, Hardy felt, didn't matter. It might still be real. In daring to feel that way, he was following directly in the steps of the American philosopher and psychologist William James (1842–1910), brother of the novelist Henry James. William James had revolutionized the scientific exploration of spiritual phenomena with his book *The Varieties of Religious Experience* (1902). In *Varieties* and other books, James made the pioneering suggestion that though it might be impossible to catch spiritual experiences and examine them in a laboratory, that doesn't mean they aren't real.

James—not surprisingly, given that he was a psychologist—was interested in hearing what people who had had unusual psychological experiences had to say and treating what they had to say seriously. Not blindly and uncritically, not within the frame of some judgmental religious dogma, but as potential pieces of the puzzle of who and what we really are. His

Varieties of Religious Experience is full of firsthand descriptions of the mystical experiences of everyone from the most revered mystics (St. Teresa of Avila, St. John of the Cross) to absolutely ordinary people. James, almost alone at the time, recognized that these very different individuals had had experiences of the spiritual dimension that were stunningly similar, both in their content and the effect they had on the people who had undergone them. Unlike the other psychologists of his day, James saw in unusual psychological/spiritual experiences not pathologies in need of fixing, but hints at greater vistas of human possibility: suggestions of what humans might next be. The "human potential movement," launched in earnest in the sixties, owes its existence in large part to him.

James had many detractors but nonetheless was a massive figure in his time. But with the arrival of the twentieth century and the aggressive turn to hard-core empirical psychology (studying rats in mazes, dissecting brains, and other such cut-and-dried pursuits), the kind of subtle explorations James had pioneered fell into disrepute. Who cared what some high-strung neurotics had to say about seeing the heavens open or speaking with spirits? Clearly they were just making it up.

Hardy was one of a half dozen brave scientific souls who, in the middle of the twentieth century, felt that the perspective James pioneered was the real future of psychology, and that forgetting about it was a disastrous mistake. Hardy was particularly interested in the experiences of a Dutch visionary named Jakob Boehme (1575–1624). One day while gazing at a shaft of sunlight reflecting off a pewter dish, Boehme experienced a vision into the structure of the world. A similar but even more intense experience happened several years later. During it, Boehme wrote, "the gate was opened to me that in one quarter of an hour I saw and knew more than if I had been many years together at a university. . . ."*

Boehme was not a dreamy-eyed mystic closeted away in a monastery. He was a shoemaker. You cannot get more this-worldly than making shoes. How could a down-to-earth individual like this make a claim to learning more in fifteen minutes than in many years at a university?

It's probably not surprising to learn that some of the local church authorities were not pleased when Boehme began writing of what was revealed to him during these moments of vision. Dogmatic religion is not open to people having direct access to those higher realms. But there have always been currents in the world's religions that *are* open to this possibility, and currents in science as well. Hardy had noticed that the average, ordinary person's life often holds these kinds of extraordinary moments, but that such people don't talk about them because they don't think they will be taken seriously. He wanted to get to the heart of what those realms are, and he was ready to take the people who had had experiences of them at their word.

This world was not vague and abstract but fantastically powerful. Hardy wrote:

---

*Quoted in Bucke, *Cosmic Consciousness*, 181–82.

The Gift of Belonging

At certain times in their lives many people have had specific, deeply felt, transcendental experiences which have made them all aware of the presence of this power. The experience when it comes has always been quite different from any other type of experience they have ever had. They do not necessarily call it a religious feeling, nor does it occur only to those who belong to an institutional religion or who indulge in corporate acts of worship. It often occurs to children, to atheists and agnostics, and it usually induces in the person concerned a conviction that the everyday world is not the whole of reality: that there is another dimension to life.*

Accounts of experiences of illumination like this—along with all kinds of others—poured into Hardy's office. It seemed that not only had many people undergone experiences like these, but many had also been waiting for someone with Hardy's background to ask about them. They were both relieved and elated that at last a genuine scientist had expressed an interest in what had happened to them. Many said to Hardy what so many people have said to me:

"I've never told anyone this before."

Dear Dr. Alexander—

I read your book on Saturday in four hours. Once I started reading I was unable to put it down.

  After living for 50 years without experiencing the death of a close family member, I began a two-year period within which

---

*Hardy, *The Spiritual Nature of Man*, 1.

I lost 7 people extremely close to me. I had been bothered by an incident which occurred during the first death, my ex-mother-in-law, Ann. My ex-husband was in Afghanistan and trying desperately to return to be by her side. It was a four-day process for him to get to the U.S. There being no other living family members (other than my daughters who we felt were too young) I was asked to be with her in case she passed before her son arrived, and immediately went to her side.

She was dying from emphysema and her mind was totally intact for being 82 years of age. She was only able to speak very softly and had to whisper in my ear to communicate. She said many things to me about incidents from many years ago. She knew her granddaughters' names. She knew her son was coming and she knew who I was. We spent the first day "re-bonding" as ten years had passed since I last saw her. She thanked me for being "the one" that was with her at that time. She was very concerned about her hair and appearance. She was wearing a red hat when I arrived and even when it appeared she was sleeping she would reach up and make sure the hat was on her head properly. She did this at least 10–15 times a day while I was there. Otherwise, she seemed to follow what I now know is a normal course of hospice-induced death. She stopped eating, then drinking, got a burst, etc.

On the day she died, around mid-morning, she asked me when her son was arriving. I told her it would be two more days and she got an instant look of anguish on her face. It said she couldn't wait that long. She pulled me close and told me that her mother and brother were there to take her (they both predeceased her) and they wanted her to go. Not knowing where the words came from, I leaned in close and whispered to her that if they were there to take her she should go, because just as she is seeing her mother and brother again, she would see her son again as well. She smiled the most peaceful smile I ever saw . . . her smile said so many things all at one time.

My daughters came that afternoon and filled her room with Christmas! She smiled that same smile as she looked around at the tree, snowman and lights they brought in. After a while they left and it was she and I again. She fell asleep for a while and so did I. I woke up around 11 pm to see my mother-in-law talking to someone at the foot of her bed. I was sitting next to her, right up towards her chest. There was no one there. She took her red hat off as if handing it to someone, then reluctantly pulled it back to herself, and then extended it again letting go and I watched it land in her lap. She smiled that smile again and leaned back and fell asleep and so did I leaving the hat there on her lap.

I awoke again around 1:00 am and the first thing I noticed was that her feet were right next to me. She had died and turned side to side in the bed while doing so. She had a very "tormented" look on her face. The hat was gone. I called a nurse. The nurses immediately went into their routine and removed her clothing, bedding, etc. and then wrapped her in a sheet and placed her back in the bed. They handed me clear Hefty bags and instructed me to start packing her things. I did. They helped.

At 2 am my ex-husband called. I spoke with him for 45 minutes. We decided to wait and tell our daughters in the morning. After hanging up the phone I was standing outside

*of her room with her things in bags only to see that it was
snowing—an extremely heavy snow fell. Living 30 minutes
away and high in the mountains I did not want to try and drive
home. My husband was out of town and I did not want to call
one of my daughters because I did not want them driving in the
storm either so I stood in the hallway feeling extremely alone, still
feeling shocked and numb pondering what to do.*

*. . . The following morning I went through my mother-in-
law's belongings at the request of her son. The red hat was gone.
I thought perhaps it had gotten wrapped up in her bedding so I
immediately called the hospice center, who immediately tracked the
laundry because everyone there knew about the red hat. She wore
it everyday all the time even while sleeping. It was never found.*

*. . . I continued to lose people. One of my closest friends died in
a motorcycle accident shortly thereafter. Then my father became
ill. I was there while he was dying. We were sitting outside his
home a few days before he died, just he and I when he looked
at me very matter-of-factly and said, "Did you just see her?" I
asked, "Who, Dad?" and he described a woman that had just
"walked by" and began describing her to me—what she looked
like, what she was wearing and I knew he was speaking of his
sister Natalie who had died when he was young—I had seen her
picture and I knew he was describing that picture.*

*So I asked him if he saw her face in hopes he would say her
name but instead he looked at me very calmly and pointed to the
front door and said, "No I didn't, but she went inside if you want
to go in and see her." That evening after I left to go and get some
sleep he told my mother that Natalie was there and was coming*

back tomorrow to "take me to church." He died the following day. During those days prior to dying he kept looking up at the ceiling and extending his arms and saying "wow" as if he was looking at the most beautiful thing he had ever seen.

Next, my Uncle Tony died. Then my new mother-in-law. I was not present with either of them. Next my Aunt Jane, who was like a mother to me, also passed. Her daughter and I were with her almost every day for several weeks. She had Alzheimer's, Parkinson's and two types of cancer. She had no idea who I was. She had not recognized her own son or daughter for almost a year prior to her death. She did not remember that she was married to Uncle Joe.

The day before she passed her daughter and I walked into her room for a visit. We were surprised to see her dressed, sitting up in a chair, and smiling. As soon as we walked in the room she began talking. She told us that Mario (my father) and Tony (my uncle) had been there and they were coming back for her tomorrow. Days earlier she was unable to tell us who they even were when shown a picture. She then spent the next 3 hours talking non-stop. It was the most she had spoken since arriving there several months earlier. She was clear and no longer confused and telling us stories about her life that made sense to us. She spoke of her husband Joe who she now knew. Towards the end of the three hours she had left us with a message about our futures. She told us that we would both be "ok" and then she asked to go to bed. Almost immediately she became foggy again. Eventually we went home and discussed that it may have been her "burst."

The following morning as soon as we awoke we were called

to "come immediately" and she passed before we arrived. When I walked into the room she had such a look of peace on her face she was almost smiling. So different than the look I saw on my mother-in-law.

Since all of these deaths have occurred I have had "strange" things happen around me. Some people call them "signs"—I do not know what to make of them and did not discuss them with anyone for fear they would think I had lost my mind. Many of these things have "haunted" me if you will. This past Saturday I walked into a store with my cousin to buy a birthday card. While she veered to the right to get a card I continued walking and did not stop until I reached the stand which held your book. I don't know why I stopped there. I picked up your book as well as the one next to it, Waking Up in Heaven, and read both of them cover to cover in one sitting. I no longer think I am crazy. While reading them I was filled with such a peace that I have not known for some time. Everything made sense.

I know this is a very long story and I apologize for taking so much of your time. I just had to tell you that your story changed my life in so many ways. I don't know why I did not go out and explore this on my own while these things were happening—I just didn't. I feared people would think I was crazy and kept my story to myself. It's different than your story but when your doctor friend talked about his experience with his father it matched mine. I truly believe that something (or someone) pulled me to your story and always will. Thank you for sharing it and for scientifically explaining that these things can and do happen. May God continue to bless you Eben Alexander—you will remain forever in my prayers.

The Gift of Belonging

In letters like these—so powerful in their heartfelt directness—I hear people telling me just what so many people told Hardy, and James before him. Experiences like these are difficult to describe not just because the tellers are worried what listeners will think, but simply because they are hard to put into words. But hard as it was, these people *did* find the words, and they wrote them out. Many told Hardy (and many have told me as well) that they simply had to.

One person explained to Hardy:

I decided to write after keeping my experience to myself for forty years. I was 16 and had always enjoyed solitary walks around my village home. One evening I set out, by myself, as usual, to walk up a lane towards the wood. I was not feeling particularly happy or particularly sad, just ordinary. I was certainly not "looking" for anything, just going for a walk to be peaceful. It must have been August, because the corn was ripe and I only had a summer dress and sandals on. I was almost to the wood when I paused, turned to look at the cornfield, took two or three steps forward so I was able to touch the ears of corn and watched them swaying in the faint breeze. I looked to the end of the field—it had a hedge then—and beyond that to some tall trees towards the village. The sun was over to my left; it was not in my eyes.

Then . . . there must be a blank. I will never know for how long, because I was only in my normal conscious mind with normal faculties as I came out of it. Everywhere surrounding me was this white, bright, sparkling light, like sun on frosty snow, like a million diamonds, and there was no cornfield, no trees, no sky, this light was everywhere; my ordinary eyes were open, but

I was not seeing with them. It can only have lasted a moment I think or I would have fallen over. The feeling was indescribable, but I have never experienced anything in the years that followed that can compare with that glorious moment; it was blissful, uplifting, I felt open-mouthed wonder.

Then the tops of the trees became visible once again, then a piece of sky and gradually the light was no more, and the cornfield was spread before me. I stood there for a long time, trying in vain for it to come back and have tried many times since, but I only saw it once; but I know in my heart it is still there—and here—and everywhere around us. I know heaven is within us and around us. I have had this wonderful experience which brought happiness beyond compare.

We see God in the miracle of life, in trees, flowers and birds—I smile when I hear talk of God as a man, wrathful or otherwise—I know I have seen and felt and am humbly grateful for the inner rock to which I cling.

*I wrote it down, but I never told anybody.**

Many of the experiences of Hardy's respondents were equally brief, but just as transformative. Another woman wrote:

My husband died on 6 September 1968 and for nearly a year afterwards I was extremely depressed and nothing, just nothing, could console me. One morning whilst sitting in my bath, too depressed to think of anything at all, there suddenly came into my head a bril-

---

*RERC account 4405, quoted in Maxwell and Tschudin, *Seeing the Invisible*.

*liant golden hue, the like of which I had never seen before, and at its base there was a small black spot about the size of a pinhead. For what must have been a few seconds I felt very frightened until at last I seemed to realize that it was my husband. I cried out to him and at once the beautiful golden hue slowly faded away and I have not seen it since. This is all that happened but it left me with a great peace of mind and a conviction that all is well. I also think that my faith has become much stronger as a result of this experience.**

Once you have had a glimpse of the higher worlds, and the sense of deep belonging that they inspire and that so much of life conspires to make us forget, all kinds of experiences can pull you back into touch with them. The fact is that many of the things people love to do, without being able to explain exactly *why* they love them, make us feel good precisely because they are reconnecting us with that world. I don't surf, but both my sons do. I've watched people surf and heard surfers talk, and I know that part of the magic of that sport is that it's an especially powerful reconnector to the worlds beyond this one: that realm where there is so much more movement, so much more life and feeling available. I love to ski, and if you've ever skied you'll know that feeling just as you start to drop down a steep slope. There's a part deep inside you that wakes up when this happens. It's physical, but it's *more* than physical.

Needless to say, this applies in spades to the feeling I got when skydiving. I now see my youthful passion for that sport

---

*RERC, account number 2389, quoted in Hardy, *The Spiritual Nature of Man*, 92.

as probably the greatest indicator that I had a hunger for heaven, even if at the time I sure wouldn't have called it that.

There's a word used by athletes—and, not coincidentally, by drug users—that's especially significant here:

Rush.

As a doctor, I know that when your body is stimulated naturally or artificially, there are very specific things going on in the brain. Every pleasure we experience when in the body is visible in the brain's neural activity, and the rush delivered by jumping out of a plane or ingesting a powerful drug both hit essentially the same centers in the brain.

The mistake here is looking at that neural activity and seeking to explain our entire conscious experience through it. We experience life through the brain while we are in our bodies. The brain is the switching station between "here" (the body) and "there" (the vast worlds beyond the body). But this doesn't mean that the brain is the *cause* of our conscious experience. What's really going on is much more complex. There's a constant back-and-forth between our brain and our consciousness, with the brain trying valiantly to keep us alive and out of harm's way, trying to retain complete control, trying not to be distracted by the very real input coming from beyond the physical world. When a drug addict makes himself or herself feel good by taking a drug, he or she is gaining a degree of release from the control that the physical brain, with its obsession with survival-related data, exercises over us. The rush a drug addict feels and the rush a surfer or skydiver feels are both momentary shifts up, out of the body's embrace. The problem with the drug user is that this method of gaining that release is a form of cheating. The brain is *forced* to give up its hold on consciousness, and when the drug wears off, the user falls back more deeply into embodiment. He hits the ground hard, and with each new departure and return he takes this way, he damages both soul and body—not to mention weakening his chances of ever being able to attain that release naturally. All rushes end, here on earth. But they don't up there. Up there, the feeling is constant. A constant rush here on earth would soon turn into a nightmare. So imagining what that feels like from our perspective is, once again, pretty much impossible. But that doesn't mean it's not true.

Many of the reports Hardy collected were recollections of experiences that had occurred far back in childhood—sometimes six or seven decades beforehand. But for the respondents, the memory of them was as fresh as if they'd occurred just a few days before.

This in itself was highly suggestive. As kids, many of us were completely at home with the idea that there was an invisible reality. We moved among invisible things, even as we negotiated the (usually) far less interesting world of adult reality. But we weren't fooled. Like me with my Superman cape, we knew full well which world was the more important one.

Then—for many people, interestingly, around the age of seven or eight—this stopped. A connection went dead, and from then on, day by day, the rules of the "adult" world took over. The Scottish poet Edwin Muir (1887–1959) wrote:

A child has a picture of human existence peculiar to himself, which he probably never remembers after he has lost it: the original vision of the world. I think of this picture or vision as that of a state in which the earth, the houses on the earth, and the life of every human being are related to the sky overarching them; as if the sky fitted the earth and the earth the sky. Certain dreams convince me that a child has this vision, in which there is a completer harmony of all things with each other than he will ever know again. *

Childhood is a time when heaven and earth are still essentially united. Later, as we grow older, they move apart—perhaps a little, perhaps a lot. But however far away it seems to get, we get hints and glimpses—and sometimes more—that heaven is really still close at hand.

"It was as if something said to me, 'Don't ever allow yourself to question this,'" Hardy associate Edward Robinson quotes one individual describing a moment of childhood spiritual insight. "And I knew that I mustn't; I knew it was the most real thing that had ever happened to me." †

"If it was [a] hallucination," Robinson quotes another individual in his book on childhood spiritual experiences saying, "why do I remember it as the most real and living experience that I have ever had? It was like contacting a live wire when you are groping for a match." ‡

---

*Robinson, *The Original Vision*, epigraph.
†Ibid., 21.
‡Ibid., 22.

As writers like William James, the classicist Frederic W. H. Myers in the late nineteenth century, and the writer Aldous Huxley in the mid-twentieth century have suggested, there is strong evidence that the brain acts as a kind of "reducing valve" for consciousness. We know more when we are "out" of the brain, that is, than we do when we are in it. Another respondent wrote to Hardy:

> *I think from my childhood, I have always had the feeling that the true reality is not to be found in the world, as the average person sees it. There seems to be a constant force at work from the inside trying to push its way to the surface of consciousness. The mind is continually trying to create a symbol sufficiently comprehensive to contain it, but this always ends in failure. There are moments of pure joy with a heightened awareness of one's surroundings, as if a great truth had been passed across. . . . At times it feels that the physical brain is not big enough to let it through.**

To those still seduced by the simplistic notion that "the brain creates consciousness"—those who might recoil when I mention that destruction of my neocortex greatly heightened my awareness—I would remind you of two commonly witnessed clinical phenomena that defy the simplistic brain-creates-mind model: 1) *terminal lucidity* (in which demented elderly patients close to death often have astonishing oases of cognition, memory, insight, and reflection as they approach death, often

---

*RERC account 000651, quoted in Robinson, *The Original Vision*, 27.

at periods when they are fully aware of departed souls there to escort them to the spiritual realm); and 2) the *acquired savant syndromes* (in which some form of brain damage—such as that seen in autism, head injury, or stroke—allows for some super-human mental capability such as advanced calculation abilities, intuition, musical abilities, or perfect memory of numbers, names, dates, or visual scenery). There is no explanation within our simplistic neuroscientific ideas of the brain to explain such extraordinary and counterintuitive observations.

As I dove more deeply into the mystery of my journey, I came to realize that our own consciousness is the only thing any one of us truly knows to exist. The neuroscience I had studied for decades would remind us that *everything* any of us has ever experienced, since before we were born, is nothing more than the electrochemical activity (frequency, vibration) of one hundred billion neurons interacting in an extraordi-narily complex three-pound gelatinous mass that we know as the human brain.

Today, the nerve center of scientific work on conscious-ness is the Division of Perceptual Studies (DOPS) at the University of Virginia, where researchers Ed Kelly and Emily Williams Kelly, Bruce Greyson, and others are working to resuscitate the massive work done by scholars like Myers and James at the turn of the nineteenth century and bring it back into the public eye. I would suggest that, if anything in this slender book sets you on fire and you find you want to go deeper, that you tackle their massive but life-changing study *Irreducible Mind: Toward a Psychology for the Twenty-first Cen-*

tury. The book is long and dense because the DOPS group are scientists, and they have sought to reply in full to the common objections to the idea that consciousness survives the death of the brain.

As human beings, we have undreamed-of potential. We are only at the very beginning of understanding who and what we truly are. The body holds countless clues to the true cosmic beings that we are in nascent form. When things are working in concert, the body is not simply an anchor and obfuscation to our spiritual realities, but a tool for bringing those capabilities to earth. So, too, we see from authenticated cases of child geniuses and prodigies, is the brain. Make no mistake: There is a reason we are spiritual beings having an earthly experience. We are here to learn, but we bring with us far greater tools to accomplish that learning than we currently realize. Our odyssey through the material isn't simply a test, and is definitely not a punishment, but is rather a chapter in the unfolding, the evolution, of the cosmos itself: for we are one of God's greatest experiments, and the Deity's hopes are pinned on us to a degree that is almost infinitely beyond our ability to imagine.

The people who responded to Hardy thirty years ago, and the people I meet and talk to every day, are saying the same thing. It's the one true story, fighting its way back to us. The reality of heaven, and of our place in it, is breaking back through the walls of denial we have built up over the last few centuries, and we are hearing its message again: We are loved. We are known. We belong.

There was yet another feeling that used to come over me, which now I can only call a kind of insight. At the same time, I only remember the feeling as one of intense reality and knowing, a sort of feeling when I really saw and knew how things really were underneath appearances. At these times of knowing I did not see quivering colours, nor feel huge, nor hear strange inner hums; but rather I saw the ordinary world very clearly and in infinite detail, and knew it to be all joined up.*

The respondent who wrote this description to Hardy was most likely not a scientist. But what this person is talking about is not dissimilar to what modern physicists are talking about when they tell us that on the physical level there is no ultimate separation of anything from anything else. Separation, at a fundamental level, does not exist in the universe, and that's the case whether one is looking at it from a scientific perspective, a psychological perspective, or both.

The experience of this connection, when it comes, is hugely powerful. But it is easily broken. Another respondent wrote to Hardy:

As I grew up, I was ever more perplexed to realize that many people lived in a world quite different from my own. They could kill things without hurting themselves, they could sleep without dreaming, or dream without colors. They could apparently always feel themselves to be inside their skins, and the things they saw and

---

*RERC account 000500, quoted in Robinson, *The Original Vision*, 28–29.

*heard and felt seemed real and separate and distinct realities. The objective world seemed real to most people, and the subjective world unreal or nonexistent.**

The initiation ceremonies of many traditional peoples occur right around the time when this initial period of childhood "innocence," of direct and uncomplicated connection with the spiritual world, comes to an end. When we lose that original childhood connection, that intuition of belonging, it's the job of religion to step in and help us get it back and keep it. Traditional societies, aware of the deep connection that children have with the spiritual side of the universe, knew exactly when it was time to do this, to help the emerging adult codify the knowledge of heaven he or she had naturally known as a child so that it would never be lost.

Were one asked to characterize the life of religion in the broadest and most general terms possible, one might say that it consists of the belief that there is an unseen order, and that our supreme good lies in harmoniously adjusting ourselves thereto.

—WILLIAM JAMES, *THE VARIETIES OF RELIGIOUS EXPERIENCE*

---

* Robinson, *The Original Vision*, 29.

Needless to say, that is what today's religions should be doing as well. But the sad but fascinating fact is that a child in an Amazonian rain forest tribe six hundred years ago got the tools he or she needed to navigate the material world and stay connected to the spiritual one, while our children often don't. This is not to denigrate Christianity or the other modern faith traditions in any way. But it is to say that those faiths need to join with each other and with science to create a new vision: one that encompasses science *and* religion, and that will teach our children real ways to stay in touch with the spiritual world at all times. We need to become a culture that, like so many that existed in the past, shows *all* its members how to hold on to the golden thread, all through their lives.*

Thomas Traherne, a seventeenth-century clergyman whose writings were only discovered by chance in the late nineteenth century, wrote that "you never enjoy the world aright till the Sea itself floweth in your veins, till you are clothed with the heavens, and crowned with the stars: and perceive yourself to be the sole heir of the whole world, and more than so, because men are in it who are every one sole heirs as well as you."

Heirs: the perfect word. From a material perspective, as we noted earlier, we are cosmic beings. The ocean literally flows in our veins, because blood is virtually identical to the salt water from which our animal bodies developed. Likewise, the calcium atoms that compose our bones and the carbon

---

*That's one reason why I've been working so hard, especially through my work with Sacred Acoustics, to develop forms of spiritual exercise that anyone today, perhaps most especially young people, can do. See the appendix.

atoms that make up 18 percent of our bodies were forged billions of years ago in the hearts of ancient stars—stars that, when they collapsed into white dwarfs and re-exploded as supernovas, blasted those atoms out into the universe, where eventually they cohered with other complex elements to form planets like this one, as well as the physical bodies of all the living beings that now live and move upon our planet. But we are also spiritual beings: the heirs of heaven. Our material heritage and our spiritual heritage aren't separate but twine together, again like those twin snakes making their way up the caduceus. From an "outside," Aristotelian perspective, we are "made" from earth. But from an inner, Platonic/initiatory perspective, we are made from celestial clay—from what the mystics of twelfth-century Persia called "the earth of heaven." We belong to both worlds.

CHAPTER 6

The Gift of Joy

*It is in moments of great joy that our true being is most visible.**
— MEDHANANDA, TWENTIETH-CENTURY GERMAN HINDU MYSTIC

The worlds above this one flow with emotion, with warmth that is more than simply physical, and with other qualities far above and beyond my ability to describe. But I can tell you this: I was ready for them. Though they struck me with a dazzling newness and freshness, they were also, paradoxically, familiar. I'd felt them before. Not as Eben Alexander, but as the spiritual being I was long, long before that particular embodied being came along, and that I will be again, when the earthly elements that currently make up my physical body have gone their different ways.

---

*Medhananda, *With Medhananda on the Shores of Infinity*, 34.

The worlds above are not general, not vague. They are deeply, piercingly alive, and about as abstract as a bucket of fried chicken, the glint off the hood of a car, or your first crush. That's why the descriptions of heaven brought back by people like Swedenborg can sound so absolutely crazy. I know perfectly well how crazy my own account sounds, and I sympathize with those who have difficulty with it. Like a lot of things in life, it sounds pretty far-fetched till you see it yourself.

There are trees in the worlds above this one. There are fields, and there are animals and people. There is water, too—water in abundance. It flows in rivers and descends as rain. Mists rise from the pulsing surfaces of these waters, and fish glide beneath them. Not abstract, mathematical fish, either. Real ones. Every bit as real as any fish you've seen, and way, way more so. The waters there are like earthly water. And yet they're not earthly water. They are, to state it in a way that I know falls short but is accurate all the same, more than simply earthly water. It's water that is closer to the source. Closer, like the water higher up on a meandering river is closer to the springs from which it emerges. It's water that's deeply familiar—so that when you see it you realize that all the most beautiful waterscapes you ever saw on earth were beautiful precisely because they were reminding you of it. It's living water, the way everything is living up there, and it pulls you in, so that your gaze wants to travel into it, deeper and deeper, on and on, forever. It was water that made all the earthly bodies of water I've seen, from Carolina beaches to western rivers, seem like lesser versions, little siblings of this, the thing that on some deep level I'd always known water should be.

That's not to denigrate the oceans and rivers and lakes and thunderstorms and all the other forms of water I've seen and enjoyed on this earth. It is, instead, simply to say that I now see these waters in a new perspective, just as I see all of the natural beauties of the earth in a similarly new one. When we ascend, in short, everything's still there. Only it's more real. Less dense, yet at the same time more intense—more *there*. The objects and landscapes and people and animals burst with life and color. The world above is as vast and various and populated and as different in one place than in another as this one is, and infinitely more so. But in all this vast variety there is not that sense of *otherness* that characterizes this world, where one thing is itself alone and has nothing directly to do with the other things around it. Nothing is isolated there. Nothing is alienated. Nothing is disconnected. Everything is *one*, without that oneness in any way suggesting homogeneity: that is, being all mashed together. The writer C. S. Lewis put this wonderfully when he pointed out that the oneness of God should not conjure up in our minds some big, bland tapioca pudding. It's not *that* kind of oneness.

To see this world for but one moment is to have your heart broken with the sudden inrushing memory of its reality. But it is also to have your heart healed, because you remember where you're from, what you are, and where you're going again, someday. You've glimpsed the world outside the cave, and all has changed, forever.

Ultra-real, frequently mentioned in descriptions of NDEs, is a key concept here. As I told my older son, Eben, who was majoring in neuroscience in college, when I was released from the hospital: "It was all *way too real to be real!*" Knowing that every time one revisits a memory one risks altering it, he advised me to write down everything I could remember about my coma odyssey before I read anything about near-death experiences, physics, or cosmology. Eight weeks later, after having written more than twenty thousand words, I delved into the NDE literature. I was astonished to find that more than half of NDE-ers report that realm to be far more real than this one. That is a hard concept to convey to skeptical materialists who have deeply buried their memories of that realm, but it is refreshingly easy to share with those who have been there—the discussion often transcends the very words that can be so limiting in our communications about such nonearthly realms (given the limitations of our earth-based language).

A curious property of memories from these deep transcendental NDEs, in addition to their strikingly ultra-real nature, is that they are persistent and life-changing. These memories do not fade as most brain-derived memories do. I've had people come up to me after presentations and offer detailed renditions of NDEs that they experienced more than seven decades earlier, as if they had happened yesterday. Further reading, not only of the NDE literature, but of the afterlife literature and the writings of religious mystics and prophets going back for thousands of years, elucidated the profound similarities in so many of these experiences. So many are trying to describe the same awesome, infinitely loving presence at the core of all being. Some skeptics miss the forest for the trees—they get lost in the details, so busy comparing the differences in their effort to disprove, that they miss the deeper truth of the commonalities across cultures, beliefs, continents, and millennia.

That realm is far more real than this murky, dreamlike material realm. The veil that I believe lies between them is cleverly constructed by an intelligence infinitely greater than our own, and it is there for a reason. This earthly realm is, I believe, where we are meant to learn the lessons of unconditional love, compassion, forgiveness, and acceptance. Our knowing of our eternal spiritual nature is not meant to be as clear to us as the moon rising in the sky at night. Our ability to fully learn the most important lessons of life depends on our being partially veiled from that more complete (yet finite) knowing that our higher souls possess between lives.

How can all this be? How can there be other worlds where we actually encounter things and situations and beings that are like those in this world? The easiest way to understand is to take a sketch of the universe used in many ancient traditions, but especially by the mystics of ancient Persia. This sketch or map sees the universe as wide at the bottom and pointy at the top—like a wizard's hat. Picture such a hat sitting on the ground. The bottom part, the wide flat circle of ground that the hat covers, is the earthly realm. Now picture the hat as having a series of floors inside it: floors that get narrower and narrower as we move up. This is a very clean (though obviously hugely oversimplified) way of describing what happens as the soul ascends the spiritual worlds. These worlds don't get smaller as we ascend. Just the opposite. They get vaster, more impossible to describe from where we are. But in a spatial sense, they *do* get smaller, because space no longer exists in the way it does here. Space becomes less important, because its ultimately illusory nature becomes more apparent. In these higher realms we experience directly what Bell's theorem, which shows how two particles at opposite ends of the universe can interact with no time delay whatsoever, tells us much more abstractly. The universe is *One*.

The realms above this one are full of vast spaces—vistas that dwarf the most sweeping and inspiring we can find anywhere here on earth. These spaces are full of objects and beings we recognize from earthly life. They are real. But the space they inhabit is a higher space than this one, so nothing works as it does here, and the second you start to describe it you run into problems. It's real, but—like matter itself when we get down to the quantum level—it doesn't behave in any kind of way that we are used to.

Traditional wisdom tells us that at the tip of the hat all extension vanishes. That point—the tip of the magician's hat—is the place where all of our earthly categories of space and time and movement, which get ever more spiritualized as we move up, vanish altogether. Beyond there is no space, no time . . . none of the markers we use where we are now.

The one thing we know here on earth that does remain above that point is love. God is love, and so are we, at our deepest level. This is not abstract love. There is no such thing. This love is harder than a rock and louder than a full orchestra and more vital than a thunderstorm and as fragile and moving as the weakest, most innocent suffering creature, and as strong as a thousand suns. This is not a truth we can adequately conceptualize, but it is one that we will all experience.

> *The barriers began to fall and one veil after another parted in my mind. From a self-centered happiness I now wanted to share it with others, first those near me, then wider, until everyone and everything was included. I felt I could now help all these people, that there was nothing beyond my power—I felt omnipotent. The ecstasy deepened and intensified. I began shouting. I knew that all was well, that the basis of everything was goodness, that all religions and sciences were paths to this ultimate reality.**

Like this respondent of Hardy's, after my NDE, when I learned to speak again, when my body and brain were functioning fully, what I mostly had to offer in my attempts to describe these spiritual worlds was a joyful enthusiasm: one that took the form of a long string of superlatives—adjectives that, the more I repeated them, the less anyone understood what I was trying to say. *Beautiful. Unearthly. Marvelous. Gorgeous.*

One day, when Ptolemy and I were going back and forth, trying to refine the story of my voyage in order to bring across to the reader how it really felt, he said: "Eben, I'm barring you

---

*RERC, account number 983, quoted in Hardy, *The Spiritual Nature of Man*, 78.

from typing or speaking the word *beautiful* one more time. It's not *doing* anything."

I totally got it. (Though anyone who has been to my talks knows I still constantly backslide.) I was back from a world that not only beggared all attempts at description but also made mincemeat of the very categories of description we use to describe earthly realities. There are infinitely more ways to feel and experience and communicate in the worlds beyond this one, and when I came back with the memory of that vastly greater catalogue of perceptions and feelings, it was like trying to describe something in three dimensions to a person who only lives in two. (This was an idea developed, by the way, by the clergyman and mathematician Edwin Abbott in his 1884 novel *Flatland*, in which a voyager to a land of three dimensions has an equally frustrating time when he returns to his two-dimensional world and tries to tell his two-dimensional friends about it.)

But no matter how hard it is to bring news of these realms down, it is absolutely key that those who have had these experiences try to do so anyway. These descriptions are the food we need today. Mapping those worlds above in a nonaggressive, humble way is a crucial part of healing both ourselves and our world. Everyone knows what tremendous amounts of doubt and despair are at work in the world right now. If you have a strong religious faith, you are most likely better off than someone who doesn't. But if you come, as I have, to see religion, spirituality, and science as partners in showing the universe as it truly is, I believe you can become even stronger.

Goethe, Fechner, Pascal, Swedenborg, and a host of other scientific minds found that strength when they allowed themselves to become spiritual minds as well. In these pioneering individuals, the earthly/outer and the heavenly/inner selves cast aside their apparent conflicts and became allies.

When this happens, we see that the universe is a profoundly orderly place both physically *and* spiritually. The order and meaning we feel at work in our minds is the same order and meaning we catch glimpses of outside in the world. And a glimpse of this order is enough to transform the dominant emotion that guides us through our day from one of sorrow to one of joy.

Natalie Sudman, author of *Application of Impossible Things*, a truly remarkable book about the NDE she experienced during the Iraq War when the Humvee she was in blew up, puts this as well as anyone:

> *Buddhists have said, "Pain is inevitable; suffering is optional." Understanding that I designed my experience from start to finish and being assured through my experiences out-of-body that my life as is has meaning and value, suffering is impossible. Even coming to consciousness in a charred truck sprayed with blood, or lying in a hospital bed curled up in a fetal position in excruciating pain, or puking my guts out from an anesthesia hangover (the worst!), or contemplating fifty years of double vision, I've been reminded of the underlying joy of being that I experienced most vividly out-of-body. This is not happiness, which seems to me to be more a response to environment and circumstance than a constant interior state. I can be depressed, fearful, worried, irritated, angry—in other*

words, unhappy, with my circumstances or environment while feel-
ing interested, curious, and even excited about the circumstances or
environment, my own creation of it, and my own actions and emo-
tions while in it. I don't always enjoy the fact that I'm in this world,
or enjoy being in this particular circumstance, but I always feel the
foundational joy of being a conscious, creative, expansive personality
exploring experience, and enjoy the humor inherent in that.*

This joy came to Natalie through her discovery of the reality of the worlds beyond. It was the same kind of discovery
that, in very different circumstances, the poet William Butler Yeats (1865–1939) made during the experience that he
describes in these lines: "I know now that revelation is from
the self, but from that age-long memoried self, that shapes
the elaborate shell of the mollusk and the child in the womb,
that teaches the birds to make their nest; and that genius is
a crisis that joins that buried self for certain moments to our
trivial daily mind."† Yeats was no stranger to moments of sudden illumination: moments when he saw earth in the light
of heaven, and understood that the "heavenly" was not only
beyond—not only out there, somewhere else, but right here,
right now, woven into the very fabric of what so often seems
like dull, ordinary existence.

My fiftieth year had come and gone,
I sat, a solitary man,

---

* Sudman, *Application of Impossible Things*, 111.
† Yeats, *The Collected Works, Vol. III*, 216–17.

The Gift of Joy

In a crowded London shop,
An open book and empty cup
On the marble table-top.
While on the shop and street I gazed
My body of a sudden blazed;
And twenty minutes more or less
It seemed, so great my happiness,
*That I was blessed and could bless.**

We walk about in a world of darkness. Then, something happens—anything from an unexpected act of kindness to the glint of light on a vase to a full-blown NDE in which we journey to another world. And suddenly, the world opens up. We see what's there behind it. We see what's been there the whole time, but that, in our world, we are uniquely blind to, because we have forgotten the tools for approaching it, for keeping it constantly in mind.

Ever since I was a teenager I had doubts about the existence of God, in the traditional Christian sense. I have had tremendous difficulty identifying with any religion, and yet I have always felt compelled to embrace something "beyond." Atheism was a commitment I was unwilling to make, so I have embraced the label "agnostic" since my teens.

. . . And yet, I felt compelled to believe in something. So much so that it was disturbing that I could not vocalize my beliefs. I felt lost.

---

*From "Vacillation," by William Butler Yeats.

I read Dr. Alexander's book and when he spoke of God being a light in the darkness, I had a rush of emotion so strong I broke into tears. In fact, I am welling up now as I write this, remembering. I have only felt this way three other times, when my children were born. I just had a feeling of certainty that what I was reading was true, was real, and suddenly I felt like a weight had lifted and that it was okay for me to not have a religion, it was okay to not have a label, it was okay to just feel what I was feeling.

There have been times since that I have felt overwhelmed by life, and previously I really had no coping skills other than an Ativan to calm me. The biggest impact reading the book has had has been that I now truly feel happy, and when things start to get crazy or too upsetting, I feel a sudden calm, and am able to put into perspective this life, and my worries and stress are suddenly easier to manage. Everything that Dr. Alexander wrote just feels so true.

I have always felt extremely upset knowing how horrific people can be towards one another. Children that are abused, torture, war, all of the terrible things on this planet that we do to one another. Knowing that this is not all there is makes me so incredibly happy.

My husband read the book as well, and has shifted away from his atheism label into a more "universe" type belief, where God is an entity somewhat like an energy force in our universe. I feel closer to him as a result of us both reading this book.

Thanks for taking the time to read this,

Christine

Why is there so much pain on earth? Here are two answers I don't agree with. They're really the Eastern and the Western version of the same (deeply wrong) idea:

1. It's all your karma. Be glad that the suffering you're enduring now is "paying" for the wrongs you committed in a past life.
2. Suffering makes you strong. As "fallen" creatures, God tests us to help us overcome our sinful nature.

I've seen too much pain in the course of my life—both on the part of suffering patients, and on the part of their suffering families and loved ones—and too much joy in the worlds beyond, to buy into either of these explanations. I believe that the being I call God/Om loves us infinitely: he does not want to "punish" us, nor does he want to "teach us a lesson" for our misdeeds. The real "explanation" for the pain and meaninglessness we so often experience on earth is, I believe, both much deeper, and much simpler.

Our world—this material world—is the place where meaning is camouflaged. It's easy to lose sight of. All material reality is made of atoms and molecules, and those molecules and atoms are in turn made of subatomic particles that are constantly moving in and out of existence. Where does an electron "go" when it moves from an inner to an outer orbit of an atom or vice versa? We don't know. What we do know is that matter does not stay in existence constantly. It shifts back and forth. But even though it does so, it is never really gone from the picture—never completely absent. We know—despite that we don't know where it goes when it's gone—that it will come back.

If you were ever in a play as a kid, you might have experienced one of those strange moments when, after getting totally lost in your character, you suddenly remembered where you were. You moved your foot and the floorboards creaked, and bang, you remembered that out there beyond the lights, there was a whole school stadium, with an audience full of people you knew, who had come to see you perform, and who wished you well.

Our lives here on earth are a little like this. There are times—moments like those described by so many people in this book—when we get an inkling of where we really are, and who we really are.

What should we do in such moments? Should we freeze, forget our lines, and not get through the rest of the play? Of course not. But for those of us engaged, as we all are, in the drama, the play, of earthly existence, that moment when the floorboards creak can be invaluable.

We must relearn how to see this world *in the light of heaven*. We must allow everything around us to shine forth with the utter individuality, uniqueness, and value that every sparrow, every blade of grass, and every person you know has, because each of those is a multidimensional cosmic being, manifesting right here and right now as a physical one.

We are in the midst of the most significant leap in human understanding in history. In two hundred years the world-view we currently live within will seem as limited and naïve to our children's children as that of a medieval peasant seems to us.

We are about to rediscover the other side of life: a side that a very deep, very hidden part of us never forgot to begin with, but that most of us keep secret from ourselves because our culture has told us to.

The world of subatomic physics is not the world of spirituality. But as the ancient hermetic document the Emerald Tablet says, "as above, so below." The different elements of our cosmos harmonize with each other. What we find "down here," we find in a different form "up there." The way that matter has of literally going in and out of existence parallels, in a strange way, the way that meaning can seem to completely disappear from our world—only to return. And when we know this— when we know that the meaning is there even when it seems most absent—then joy, the kind of joy Natalie Sudman talks about in that beautiful quote above, can become a constant undertone of our lives, no matter what is happening.

Dear Dr. Alexander,

My daughter Heather was born in 1969 with severe cerebral palsy. She never sat up or spoke, although she showed awareness of everything around her. She laughed often, oh did she laugh. Told by doctors she wouldn't live past 12, she died at the age of 20 in 1989. A day after she died, as I was mowing the lawn to get my mind off of her death, I was literally surrounded by Monarch butterflies that came out of nowhere. A sign of spiritual life? I don't know.

*Fast forward to 1995. In bed for the evening and still fully
awake, I asked: "How can there be a God who let this happen?"
Instantly a glowing, all white figure appeared on the left side of
the room. It was my daughter. She pointed at me and shouted: "No
daddy, you are wrong! Look!" she said pointing to the right side of
the room. A rolling cloud of bright, white light engulfed the room.
I instantly knew a few things with no words spoken at all. It is
hard to describe the feelings of euphoria I had. I knew she was okay
and an angel of God. I knew we all are okay with what's ahead
after death. I knew how small we are compared to our Creator
and our intelligence is so low as to be laughable. I know it was real
and when someone asks me "Do you believe in God?" I answer:
"No, I don't just believe, I know without a doubt."*

I don't believe; I know.

—CARL JUNG, WHEN ASKED, TOWARD

THE END OF HIS LIFE, IF HE BELIEVED IN GOD

"All manner of thing shall be well," wrote the fourteenth-
century anchoress Julian of Norwich. But "all shall be well" is
not the same as "everything is peachy." It does not mean the
world is without its terrors and sufferings. It means that we can
navigate this world if we remember one thing: that beneath
its apparent meaninglessness, there is a world of meaning that
is rich beyond all imagining. A meaning that completely en-

compasses the suffering we see all around us, and that, when we return to the world beyond this one, will once again overwhelm it.

Jung hung over the doorway to his home this quotation from the fifteenth-century Dutch theologian Desiderius Erasmus: "Bidden or unbidden, God is present." In the dimensions above time and space as we experience them here, all the heartaches and agonies and confusions of this life have already been healed. Good luck understanding that. You can't. Not completely. Not from this level. But you can get a glimpse of it. And in fact, we get those glimpses all the time. We just need to remember that we are allowed to be open to them—to know what, on a deep level, we knew anyhow.

> *My daughter Joan was killed by a car when she was 7 years old. She and I were very close and I was grief-stricken. She was lying in her coffin in her bedroom. I fell on my knees by the bedside. Suddenly I felt as if something a bit behind me was so overcome with pity that it was consolidating itself. Then I felt a touch on my shoulder lasting only an instant, and I knew there was another world.**

Meaning is here, always. But it is easy, perhaps easier here where we are than anywhere else in the universe, to lose sight of this fact. Sometimes, often when things are at their dark-

---

*RERC account number 165, quoted in Fox, *Spiritual Encounters with Unusual Light Phenomena: Lightforms*, 26.

est, the world beyond will speak to us, using the language, the symbols, of this world: sometimes as loud as lightning, sometimes as softly as the tap of a beetle on a window. And with it, our joy in life returns—a joy that can be here inside us, as Natalie Sudman says, in spite of the pain of the world, not instead of it.

CHAPTER 7

The Gift of Hope

The inner world has its clouds and rains, but of a different kind.
Its skies and suns are of a different kind. This is made apparent
only to the refined ones: those who are not deceived by the
seeming completeness of the ordinary world.
—JALAL AL-DIN RUMI, TWELFTH-CENTURY PERSIAN MYSTIC

As human beings we are creatures of time. We live in time as fish live in water, so immersed in it that we scarcely notice it, save at the more superficial levels, where we are, of course, slaves to it. Yes, we know we are late for a meeting, but we don't know, or stop to truly grasp, that thought itself cannot unfold without a time element. Nor speech, nor human interaction, nor anything else. The world as we experience it now is built from time, in combination with space. This truth is not lessened by the fact that, from the perspective of the dimensions above this one, linear time reveals itself as an illusion, just as everyday Euclidean space does as well.

Because on earth we live and act within the element of linear time, a world without a future to look forward to seems like an awful one. Think back to when you were a teenager—to those years when it seemed like new experiences were never going to stop. If you're like a lot of people, you might have noticed that at a certain point those experiences stopped arriving at quite so fast and furious a rate. Perhaps, you might have thought, the time of real growth and change was done.

Before my NDE, I had those thoughts myself. The thrill of living wasn't gone, exactly. I loved my family and my work, and there were certainly still many challenges and adventures lying ahead that I was looking forward to. But all the same, something—a kind of inner feeling of expansion, of genuine newness coming at me fast—*had* stopped. There were only going to be so many more new experiences. And they wouldn't be new—stunningly, electrifyingly new—as they once had been. I knew the limits of the world. I would never step out of another open plane door at twenty-eight hundred feet for the first time. Never feel the new rushing at me like that. I had, in short, lost hope, for that is what hope is: a sense that something truly good and truly new is on the way, right now.

Then something new happened.

You might say that my life re-blossomed. Countless poems tell us that in life we are like flowers, blossoming like they do, but fading and dying as they do as well. We grow and flower in youth, shine for a brief passing moment with the perfection of beauty and youth and life . . . and then fade and die.

Or do we? Just as flowers symbolize the apparent tragedy and transience of life, they also symbolize what lies behind that apparent transience. Everything in life has a heavenly component, but some things are more heavenly than others, and by this scale the flower is right at the top. Dante closed the *Divine Comedy* with a description of the Empyrean, the highest heaven in his cosmology, as a white rose. The Buddha likened consciousness to the lotus, a water flower that rises from the mud and murk down at the bottom of a pond and blooms on the water's surface miraculously clean and white. The Buddha's most famous sermon was one in which he said nothing, but held up a flower.

Human beings have, since deep in prehistory, used flowers to mark our key human moments. Flowers are present at beginnings (births, graduations, weddings), and also at endings (funerals). We use them at these "punctuation" times, because in times past people knew that the most crucial thing to remember at such times is the reality of the worlds above. Like us, flowers are rooted in the earth. But they remember where they came from, following the sun across the sky each day. But most important of all, flowers burst into bloom. That bursting is perhaps the most perfect earthly symbol of the completeness for which all of us yearn, and which comes into full existence only in the dimensions beyond this one.

Dear Dr. Alexander,

In October of 2007 my 18-year-old son Ben was diagnosed with an ependymoma glioma. He died 5 months later. The reason for

*this note is that during his last 3 days here . . . he went into a
coma. As a mother watching her son die, well it's obviously the
most excruciating experience bar none in my journey here. . . .
[W]e had Ben home from the hospital. His bed was in our master
bedroom. . . . Someone was always holding him even before he
went into the coma; this was the arrangement. He was never
to be alone, so my biological brother and sister, my daughter, my
husband and myself switched all night long, someone always
laying right next to him and holding him.*

*That first night I had a dream—very vivid, not a dream
state but an experience. Before I dozed I was holding onto
Ben and crying out to God, I was so desperate and angry and
confused. Well, in this dream or rather experience I was taken
up quickly into a dark but light heaven and all was calm and
all I felt was love. It was crisp and clear, very real. I knew I
was with God. . . . I looked around me and saw pieces of earth,
little patches of earth falling around me, and I asked, "What is
the meaning?" and in my spirit I heard or knew, this is what is
happening to Ben right now as his earthly body becomes less. . . .
In an instant I was sitting up in bed. And knew he was already
in the heavenly realm. He died 2 days later.*

That essential human problem—the loss of newness and
hope—was solved for me in the worlds above this one. Worlds
that, in their initial stages, are full of the familiar things of
earth, only richly and strangely changed: strangely new. As I
gazed at the flowers I saw in the world beyond, they seemed
to bloom again and again. How can flowers, which on this

level blossom and fade, be in constant bloom? They can't on this level, because here we are completely immersed in straight linear time, or the illusion of such time. Here, flowers blossom and die, just as people are born, grow old, and die as well. Hence all those libraries of novels and poems about the sadness of life—of the tragedy of how we start out young and strong and fresh, and then live and maybe learn some lessons, but die before we can do anything but pass on a few hints to our children so that they can go through the whole thing themselves.

What a tragedy!

And indeed it is, if we keep our vision confined to this world alone, and believe that all the growth and change that we experience here isn't what it really is: but one chapter of a much larger story. Our culture is obsessed with youth because we have lost the ancient knowledge that growth never stops. We are not transient, momentary mistakes in the cosmos— evolutionary curiosities that rise like mayflies, swarm for a day, and are gone. We are players who are here to stay, and the universe was built with us in mind. We reflect it, with our deepest loves and loftiest aspirations, just as it reflects us. "As above, so below."

When we return to those worlds above after the end of an individual lifetime, something very interesting happens— something one sees constantly in the NDE literature. People talk about the "greeters," the people they've known from life who are there to welcome them. Again and again, it's the same thing. "Dad was there, but it wasn't like when he was sick.

He was young and well again." "I saw Grandma, but she was young."

How can this be? When we drop this body that we've been living and learning in, we don't vanish directly into those highest regions that we can't even begin to talk about from where we are here. We go to where I went in my own NDE. It's a "place" (it's not a place in the physical universe, but we're used to paradox by now) where we take on once again the entire life that we lived linearly down here, all at once. And what that produces, when someone else, another soul, sees it, is that person at their absolute, glowing best. If a person has lived a long time, they might appear physically in the full glow of their youthful beauty, but at the same time, they'll be manifesting the wisdom of their later years. The people we are in the world above this one are multidimensional beings: beings who contain all the best of what they were here on earth *at the same time*. If you have a grown child, think about all the different beings he or she has been over the years: The baby that first opened its eyes at the hospital, the five-year-old rolling her first few solo feet on her new bike. The teenager, suddenly revealing a thoughtfulness and depth that you had never seen before.

Which of these is your real child? You know the answer, of course. All of them are.

Life in linear time—earth time—allows for growth precisely because it takes detours and meets roadblocks. The time of heaven—the time dimension that we enter when we leave this body—allows for the full expression of those selves that we worked so hard to develop through those detours and roadblocks, here within the bonds of linear temporality. Not by "suffering because it's good for us," or by paying back past karma, but by engaging directly with the maddening opacity and limitedness that define this world. One of the most central insights of all the world's faiths is that no suffering takes place within the world without God being completely involved in it, and in fact suffering infinitely more than we do, as it is fruition and fulfillment that God desires from us, and suffering is, in some completely mysterious way, a by-product of that staggering future fulfillment. The "unlived lines" that the poet Rainer Maria Rilke said he saw on the faces of the people he passed in the street—these lines of possibility, of growth, that are so horrifically blocked and broken down here—will all have a chance to be fulfilled in the world above this one.

One of the oldest jokes about surviving bodily death is that it would be dull to live forever. The cliché image attached to this is of a group of bored people sitting around on some clouds with not a thing to do. Down below in hell, one imagines, at least the devils are having some fun.

I love this cliché, because it states precisely what the worlds beyond this one are *not*. If there is one word that describes those worlds, it is movement. Nothing holds still there for a moment. On earth, you're either on your way somewhere, or you're holding still. In the worlds beyond this one, movement and arrival become joined. The joy of travel, and the joy of arrival, meet and mingle.

This is not really as outrageous as it sounds, if you remember that physics has now demonstrated beyond any reasonable doubt that this rock-solid, physical world that you and I are inhabiting right now is, in fact, largely empty space, and that the infinitesimally small amount of matter in it is itself just a particularly dense configuration of strings of energy vibrating in a higher-dimensional space-time. But it is still hard to see, because meaning hides down here. It hides much less the higher we go in the worlds beyond this one. There things become all kinds of different things at once, so that when we use the flat-world language of earth to describe them, we immediately risk sliding into nonsense.

So it was that when I looked down, while riding on that butterfly that was symbolic yet real, with that girl who was also symbolic yet real, I saw not only flowers that bloomed and bloomed again, but people. And they were doing something that was analogous to what those perpetually blooming flowers were doing.

They were dancing.

Like music, dance is an ancient activity, its origins going deep into the very beginnings of human life on the planet. And like every primary human activity, it reflects the primary cosmic reality—that of the worlds above from which we come. When people dance, they are acting from that part of themselves that knows and remembers where it comes from and where it's going. That knows this world is not the end. That's why people dance at weddings—that earthly ceremony in which the union of two people evokes the larger union of heaven and earth. If the flower is perhaps the most heavenly object we have here on earth, dancing is perhaps the most heavenly activity. And both point to the same truth: the larger life we hope for is real.

Dancing, like singing, like music, is temporal. You can't have dancing or music without time. In the world I entered during my days in coma, there was music and there was dancing. So again, there was time—or rather, the *deep time* of those worlds. It was *a richer, more spacious kind of time* than we experience here on earth.

The Christian philosopher Thomas Aquinas had a word for this time-above-time that I encountered. He called it "aeveternity"—the time of the angels. He did not believe this was an abstract state, but rather a very real and very active one. This is a kind of time in which flowers bloom, and bloom again. And where the music and dancing never stop.

The myths and legends of indigenous peoples all over the world, from the Australian Outback to the rain forests of Brazil, describe lands beyond death where dancing, and other human activities that we know here on earth, go on forever. The Aborigines of Australia call this place the Dreamtime, and they assert that this is the state humans came from and that they will return to after death. These places, I suspect, are all the same place. Shamans have been visiting it for at least thirty thousand years, just as NDE and out-of-body journeyers visit it today. It's the place that we all came from, and the place that we will all return to, intermittently when our journey of individual life ends, and permanently when this current cycle of creation comes to an end.

If it even ends then. For the Hindus feel that the worlds rise and fall forever, each new cycle of creation being a breath of Brahma, God. When Brahma exhales, a new cycle comes into being. When he inhales, all returns to where it came from. For those who believe in reincarnation (the scientific evidence of past-life memories in children is overwhelming), this process could certainly be seen as going on beyond a single life. In this scenario, all the "yous" that your present life contains (child, teenager, adult) become a subset of that still larger "you" that moves from lifetime to lifetime, incarnating again and again, growing and evolving along with the universe. This "you" at the end of the reincarnational journey contains all the identities that you ever were down here on earth, and all those identities that you have ever had, back through time past knowing. As the psychologist Christopher Bache writes in his book *Dark Night, Early Dawn*: "Now we see that our unique way of experiencing life, our singular individuality, has emerged out of an ocean of time so vast as to be almost immeasurable and that it can continue to develop for as long again still. Death is but a pause that punctuates the seasons of our life, nothing more. This insight brings us to the threshold of a new understanding of human existence."*

Just as our life is a journey that encapsulates all the different people we become as we move from youth to adulthood to old age within this single life, there is a larger, cosmic journey that each of us is on, in which we grow and change much

---

*Bache, *Dark Night, Early Dawn*, 41.

more radically than we do in just this single earthly life. Yet at the core of this vast journey, there is a single journeying being, who at the end of this cosmic cycle will be able to recall all the guises, all the joys and sorrows, all the staggering adventures that it went through as it went from life to life. This state is so far above, so far ahead, so far beyond anything we can grasp from where we are, that I feel like I'm overstepping by even trying to describe it. It was hard enough describing what heaven is like in its closer levels. But it's enough to have even the slenderest, dimmest conception of this future that is far down the line yet right here with us now as well. Now that I know there are other waters, other skies, that there are earth-like landscapes in dimensions above this one, each with its flowering meadows or thundering waterfalls or peaceful fields alive with animals and people, and that each of these worlds is more beautiful and subtle and diaphanous than the last, it only makes me love and appreciate their earthly equivalents all the more. Why? Because I now see where these earthly phenomena come from—the higher reality they easily and naturally relate to, in that "as above, so below" way that all the phenomena of the higher worlds relate to this one. And especially because I know that what unites all these worlds, the golden thread that keeps us connected no matter how far away we get, is love.

From time to time I have again experienced these wonderful ecstasies, always at completely unexpected times, sometimes while washing up and doing daily chores about the house. There is

*always this same feeling, leaving me weeping with a great joy
and feeling of deep reverence and worship and love. I think it
best described as a sort of homesickness, a "nostalgia for some other
where," almost as if I had known an existence of such beauty
and indescribable happiness and am yearning and homesick
for it again. . . . Even when everything seems to have fallen
away and troubles pile up and I've thought that doubt was the
only certainty, rock-bottom of despair, as comes to everybody;
even then this yearning for something I had known somewhere
sustains and brings me through. Could it be a self-evident sort
of truth? One can't be homesick for something one has never
known.***

As one ascends the levels of the worlds beyond this one,
the landscapes become less crowded, less populated with
things familiar, yet at the same time all the *more* familiar.
Only it's a different kind of familiarity you feel in these
higher worlds—a more challenging one, because the realities you are coming back into contact with have been further
away from you for longer than the lower ones have. Yet at the
same time, these higher realities strike you in a deeper place,
because the higher in the worlds you go, the deeper the part
of yourself that is being called out. At our very center, deep
beneath the surface character we have built up in the course
of this lifetime, there is a part of us so central, so timeless, and
so fundamental that mystics have been politely disagreeing

---

*RERC, account number 975, quoted in Hardy, *The Spiritual Nature of Man*, 60.

for centuries as to whether it is the place where we intersect with God, or whether it is God itself. My understanding is that Eastern religions generally equate this deepest and most central part of us directly with the Divine, while Western religions tend to keep a distinction between the individual soul or self and God. One thing I am sure of is that we should respect what the highest practitioners of *all* the traditions have to tell us, and remember that when we speak in ordinary, everyday language about these realms we are here trying to map and understand, we are always to one degree or another like children talking about things they are too young to understand.

But one thing we *can* understand from our perspective, whether just abstractly or directly, is that the higher in the spiritual worlds we go, the deeper into our selves we go as well, so that in the end we discover that not only are we much huger than we ever imagined, but so too is the universe with which we are completely, wonderfully, and inextricably connected.

When the mystics say that earthly objects are not "real," that they do not possess any underlying substantiality, they are not denigrating those objects at all, but in a way are actually *venerating* those objects by showing where they actually come from. Physical matter is the child of the spiritual realms; all reality that this world has, it owes to the worlds above. But because all the worlds do symbolize and connect with each other, the objects around us—even the most passing and ephemeral—do have a claim to reality, because this world, low as it is, is nonetheless connected to those higher worlds.

So nothing down here—and certainly no living being—is orphaned. Nothing is totally lost forever.

Lao Tzu, the founder of the Chinese religion of Taoism, said the Tao is like a great womb that produces everything, yet contains nothing. The Buddha described true reality as emptiness: an emptiness that is at the same time not empty at all, but full beyond all comprehension. These men were describing the higher regions of the heavens; hence the level of paradox in their utterances is at its highest, for the higher we go the more paradoxical things become.

Hard as these concepts are to grasp from where we are, and as different as the maps of the spiritual domains charted by the world's religions can sometimes seem, I am coming to understand that at their highest point all these traditions agree. As a scientist who has caught a glimpse of the world of spirit, I believe they simply *have* to, because like a mountain with a thousand paths leading up it, all the worlds come from and end in one place only: that center of centers, that peak of peaks, and that heart of hearts that I call, knowing the word does it no justice, the Divine.

Dear Dr. Alexander,

I experienced something that I have not heard of before or after.
    As a bit of background . . . My father, a former Korean War POW, was dying of a massive pulmonary embolism in hospice at the VA. Just when we thought it was over, he began breathing deeply, deliberately and loudly and he kept this up for more than

*24 hours. The nurses told us that war veterans have a different
dying experience than others because of combat training and the
way they are programmed to never ever give up.*

*We were very close. Well, at one point I just knew that it was
the end, and I automatically held his left hand, then placed my
right hand so that I was straddling his carotid artery and chest
to feel when his heart and breathing stopped. I closed my eyes to
pray, when quite abruptly I was thrown into what I can only
describe as a cross between a movie and a dream, though it was
extremely vivid. I hovered in back and over him much like a
cameraman—there but not participating.*

*He was struggling to hold onto some rocks on the side of a
swiftly moving stream and was clearly exhausted and terrified.
Suddenly the attention of both of us was caught by a yellow
white glow above the middle of the stream, which illuminated a
white canoe with a red paddle sitting motionless on the moving
water. With a kind of cry my Dad let go of the rocks and swam
swiftly to the canoe and vaulted into it as the fit man he was in
his 20's and 30's. I zoomed with him and ended up just behind
his head. He began paddling vigorously and just once looked
back at me with a look of what can only be described as joy on his
face. It was so far beyond what I can describe that its power and
radiance can still overwhelm me.*

*It lasted just a moment. Then he turned back and resumed
enthusiastically paddling away. He turned a corner, went
behind some trees, and I was left behind. And I thought well,
that's it. But suddenly, as if I were attached to a rubber band,
I was catapulted to the top of a tree off to the left and at a little*

distance. There below, on kind of a U-shaped dock was a crowd of people who did not see me. The faces were all blurry but I recognized family members and old friends of his by their bodies. My Dad came paddling into view from the right, and, as soon as they saw him, the crowd began shouting his name and cheering in welcome. He seemed beside himself with pleasure, grinning, and almost a little stunned at first. Then he jumped out of the canoe with his paddle raised in kind of a victory salute and disappeared into the embraces and backslaps of the crowd. . . .

Boom—I was back at his bedside. Just as I began to open my eyes I felt his last pulse and breath. It is still as vivid in my mind as the day it happened nearly 4 years ago. I can recall every detail [in the vision], from the clothes he was wearing, to the kind of trees, to the names of the people in front waiting for him. And I can still see both the exhaustion and fear on his face while he was holding on and the way his face became illuminated with that last smile he gave me. I felt that he allowed me to accompany him partway to his afterlife. Although I was an observer and not a participant, this experience was still transformative and a gift from my Dad I could never repay. I can actually feel MYSELF glowing and am always emotional when I tell this story.

Again, I have never heard any tales like this, but of course this changes nothing for me. It was the most amazing and unexpected thing I have ever experienced, as well as one of the most valuable gifts that I have ever received.

Be ahead of all parting.

—RAINER MARIA RILKE

The people we are through all our lifetimes will one day be gathered together, into a being who combines all the beings we have ever been throughout this cosmic cycle, and that being will keep growing and growing until it finally becomes the godlike being each of us is destined to become. At this endpoint we will all be in the "sky," as we remember the word *heaven* really means, as part of the body of God.

So those perennially blooming flowers I saw—those blooms that were all movement, yet at the same time all stillness—those gave me my most powerful inkling of what we ourselves are as we move toward that point of incalculable perfection that lies "ahead" from one perspective, yet which is also, paradoxically enough, right here and right now.

Here is an account, from his wife, of the last days of the film critic Roger Ebert before he succumbed to cancer:

On April 4, he [Ebert] was strong enough again for me to take him back home. My daughter and I went to pick him up. When we got there, the nurses were helping him get dressed. He was sitting on his bed, and he looked really happy to be going home. He was smiling. He was sitting almost like Buddha, and then he just put his head down. We thought he was meditating, maybe reflecting on his experiences, grateful to be going home. I don't remember who noticed first, who checked his pulse. . . . In the beginning, of course, I was totally freaked out. There was some kind of code thing, and they brought machines in. I was stunned. But as we realized he was transitioning out of this world and into the next, everything, all of us, just went calm. They turned off the machines, and that room was so peaceful. I put on his music that he liked, Dave Brubeck. We just sat there on the bed together, and I whispered in his ear. I didn't want to leave him. I sat there with him for hours, just holding his hand.

Roger looked beautiful. He looked really beautiful. I don't know how to describe it, but he looked peaceful, and he looked young.

The one thing people might be surprised about—Roger said that he didn't know if he could believe in God. He had his doubts. But toward the end, something really interesting happened. That week before Roger passed away, I would see him and he would talk about having visited this other place. I thought he was hallucinating. I thought they were giving him too much medication. But the day before he passed away, he wrote me a note: "This is all an elaborate hoax." I asked him, "What's a hoax?" And he was talking about this world, this place. He said it was all an illusion. I thought he was just confused. But he was not confused. He wasn't visiting heaven, not the way we think of heaven. He described it as a vastness that you can't even imagine. It was a place where the past, present, and future were happening all at once.

It's hard to put it into words. I just loved him. I loved him so much, I think I thought he was invincible. To tell you the truth, I'm still waiting for things to unfold. I have this feeling that

we're not finished. Roger's not finished. To me, Roger was magic.
He was just magic. And I still feel that magic. I talk to him, and
he talks back.*

It's fascinating, and always deeply moving to me, how people on the verge of leaving this world can—often after long and terrible suffering—suddenly catch a glimpse of where they are going, and of where they have actually been the whole time they were here. Ebert, a man who had made his living by words, wrote his wife a few words giving her what I am sure he felt was the most valuable gift he could possibly leave her: the truth about this world.

Ebert is right. This world *is* an illusion—a hoax. It's not real. And yet of course at the same time it *is* real, and wonderful, and deserving of our deepest love and attention. We just must not forget that it is not all there is.

All the world's a stage,
And all the men and women merely players.
—WILLIAM SHAKESPEARE

Aldous Huxley, a writer who died in 1963 after a long and painful struggle with cancer, dictated his final essay (a piece

---

*This account by Chaz Ebert appeared in *Esquire* in December 2013.

about Shakespeare commissioned by a magazine) to his wife just a few days before he passed on. In that essay, Huxley said something remarkably similar to what Ebert wrote in that note to his wife.

"The world is an illusion," Huxley said. "But it is an illusion which we must take seriously, because it is real as far as it goes." We must, Huxley argued, "find a way of being in this world while not being in it." Because in truth, we are never fully, completely here to begin with. We come from, and are destined to return to, elsewhere. When we think we are our brains and bodies and nothing more, we lose the ability to be true protagonists—true heroes. And as Joseph Campbell pointed out again and again, we are all heroes. The word *protagonist* comes in part from the Greek word *agon*, which means "contest." The word *agony*, of course, also comes from it, and it is hard to deny that life is an agonizing struggle— for some people most of the time, for most people some of the time. But it's a struggle that leads somewhere. With the contest, the *agon,* of his earthly life completed, Huxley departed, leaving behind the one piece of information we have to remember on this level, just as Ebert did. This world is not all there is. There is a larger one, of which this seemingly complete earthly world is the tiniest slice. That larger world is ruled by love, and we are all on our way home to it, so we should never despair.

Because what we lost we can have back.

The end of our journey, the place where we are going, is not a place that can be described in words. Not fully. "The opposite of a correct statement," the physicist Niels Bohr said, "is a false statement. The opposite of a profound truth may well be another profound truth."* Bohr is saying that when you get deep enough in, things no longer work on a tidy *either this or that* principle. They work on a *both this and that* principle. A particle is a particle *and* a wave. One thing is true *and* its opposite is true. We are seamlessly one with our creator, *and* we are separate beings. We are one with the universe, *and* we are individuals. Time moves forward, *and* it stays still. A particle is on one side of the universe . . . yet, at exactly the same moment, it is on the other side as well. But because the worlds are in truth all one world, we can use the words and symbols of this earth to *try* to describe it. So we say it will be something like a dance; something like a wedding; something like a flower; something like the sound of running water; and something like the glint of gold.

I can't describe it any better. But I know it's there. And I know it is our job, as a culture, to help all our members, from the very youngest to the very oldest, to remember this fact. To keep the knowledge of the reality of the worlds above this one alive at every moment. I want that woman in the nursing home, who gazed into the deep and dazzling darkness of her new husband's eyes so many years ago, to know that her husband lives still, and that she and he, and all the people and animals she ever loved, will be joined once again in that world beyond.

---

*Quoted in Delbrück, *Mind from Matter*, 167.

In one of his books, Henry Corbin, the scholar of Islamic mysticism, tells of an exchange that happened in the fifties, at a conference of religious scholars. It was during lunch. Corbin and another scholar were talking with Daisetz T. Suzuki, the famous Japanese scholar of Zen Buddhism. Corbin asked Suzuki what his first encounter with Western spirituality had been. To his surprise, Suzuki told him that years before, he had translated four books by Emanuel Swedenborg into Japanese.

Corbin and his friend were surprised. A scholar of Zen Buddhism not only reading the work of a seventeenth-century scientist and Christian visionary, but going to the work of translating him into Japanese? They asked him what similarities he found between Swedenborg and Zen.

Corbin writes: "I can still see Suzuki suddenly brandishing a spoon and saying with a smile: 'This spoon *now* exists in Paradise. We are now in Heaven.'"*

I love this story. A scholar and mystic from the East celebrates a scholar and mystic from the West using the most ordinary, humdrum object one could ask for.

Wherever you are, you are in heaven now, just as is every last, most humble, most seemingly insignificant object and creature and person around you. Not in some vague, hard to understand, theoretical way, but in the most solid and real way imaginable. Real, as that respondent to Alister Hardy wrote, as grabbing a live wire. Every object you see in the world around

---

*Corbin, *Alone with the Alone*, 354.

you exists in a hierarchy of worlds, and does so at every second. That includes the nozzle of the gas pump you used when you last filled up, and the crushed plastic cup by your foot that you stared at idly as the tank filled. Heaven is here. But we have trained ourselves not to see it, and that is why so much of our world is beginning to resemble hell.

Why, back in my skydiving days, did my friends and I jump from airplanes miles above the earth, coordinating our free fall to join up for a few glorious seconds to form stars, snowflakes, or some other formation in the sky?

Well, it was *fun*. But there was something else at work, too—a kind of "just right" feeling I'd get when I'd reach out and, for a moment, all of us would succeed in creating one of those formations in the sky. During the seconds when we were joined together in free fall, we were a complete, harmonious gathering above the earth. It's funny—and yet not funny at all—that when, back in my skydiving days, my friends and I would jump out of airplanes to form those brief groupings in the sky, they would so often be circular in shape. The circle, as Plato knew, is the symbol of wholeness—of heaven and earth united, as they once were and one day will be again. And on some level, as we rocketed down through the sky and maneuvered so that for a few wonderful moments we could connect in those larger shapes, we knew this. We knew, my friends and I, as we made these circles in the sky that were such wonderful symbols of our cosmic destiny, exactly what we were doing. On a deep level, all of us know exactly what we're doing at every moment. But that knowledge pops up and sinks, pops up and sinks again. That's why we have to work so hard—harder today than ever before—to remember. We have never been this far away.

But the trip out is ending, and the trip back is beginning. That's why, when I think back to those jumps, I also always think of the first jump I made—the jump that initiated me into that heavenly brotherhood, and the question my jump-master asked me as I stood at the edge of the door getting ready to jump into the nothingness. I think of that three-word question my instructor asked me, that so many other initiates have been asked over history, and long before. Three words that our entire culture is being asked, right now, by the worlds beyond, as we prepare to enter what will be the most challenging and most wonderful chapter in our history.

Are you ready?

Acknowledgments

During my fantastic odyssey since returning from coma in November 2008, I have been blessed with the assistance, insight, and encouragement of thousands of souls from all around the globe, whose countless letters, emails, and conversations have brought me strength and conviction. My heartfelt gratitude goes out to all of them (especially to those whose stories are included in this book).

My sister Phyllis Alexander has been a tremendous blessing to me and to others by helping to foster a heartfelt connection with the souls who reach out to me. My niece Dayton Slye has also helped with this ongoing endeavor.

Karen Newell, my soul partner at all levels, for sharing her passion and knowledge and helping to bring the love that we all are into the reality of this world, to change it forever into a far better place.

My extraordinary literary agent, Gail Ross, and her associates, Howard Yoon, Dara Kaye (who, along with my sister Phyllis, has been greatly responsible for making my hectic schedule manageable), Anna Sproul-Latimer, and others at the Ross Yoon Agency.

Priscilla Painton, vice president and executive editor, and

Acknowledgments

Jonathan Karp, executive vice president and publisher, Hadley Walker, Anne Tate Pearce, and so many of their associates at Simon & Schuster for their extraordinary vision, passion, and hard work to make this world a better place.

My coauthor, Ptolemy Tompkins, for his grand knowledge, insight, and writing skills.

Raymond and Cheryl Moody, Bill Guggenheim, John Audette, Edgar Mitchell, Elizabeth Hare, Bob Staretz, Gary and Rhonda Schwartz, and many others who have helped develop Eternea.org to educate the public about the physics of consciousness and the convergence of science and spirituality.

Bruce Greyson, Ed Kelly, Emily Williams Kelly, Jim Tucker, Ross Dunseath, and all of the scientists at the Division of Perceptual Studies at the University of Virginia, for their courageous work taking modern science into far grander knowing.

Numerous additional friends whose acts of love and caring have contributed greatly during my journey: Jody Hotchkiss, Chuck Blitz, Ram Dass, Gary Zukav and Linda Francis, Kevin and Catherine Herrmann Kossi, Alexandre Tannous, Anita and Danny Moorjani, Michael and Margie Baldwin, Virginia Hummel, Bharat Mitra and Bhavani Lev, Debra Martin and Sheri Getten, Larry Dossey, Pim van Lommel, Gary Gilman, Michael and Suzanne Ainslie, Joni Evans, Mary Wells Lawrence, Terre Blair Hamlisch, Judith Caldwell, Alex and Jean Trebek, Terri Beavers, Jay Gainsboro, Ryan Knighton, and so many others.

Most of all, to my dear family for their unbounded love

and continued support in helping me come to a better under-standing of it all: my heaven-sent sons, Eben and Bond; my beloved parents, Betty and Eben Alexander Jr.; my sisters Jean, Betsy, and Phyllis; my former wife, Holley Bell Alexander; my loving birth family; and especially my departed birth-sister, also named Betsy, whom I never met in this world. She con-tinues to help millions with her loving soul.

My gratitude, most especially to God, is beyond any pos-sible words.

—Eben Alexander

Working with Eben has been one of the great adventures of my life. In addition to him and our wonderful editor, Priscilla Painton, I'd like to express my gratitude to Kate Farrell, Jerry Smith, Gene Gollogly, Art Klebanoff, Terry McGovern, Karl Taro Greenfeld, Bill Manning, Alexander Vreeland, Sydney Tanigawa, Sophia Jimenez, Steve Sittenrich, Phil Zaleski, Ralph White, Chris Bamford, Richard Ryan, Richard Smoley, Oliver Ray, Bokara Legendre, Michael Baldwin, Elise Wiarda, Dave Stang, Gary Lachman, Mitch Horowitz, Godfrey Cheshire, Rene Goodale, Robin and Stuart Ray, Christie Robb, and especially my wife, Colleen, and my stepdaughters, Evie, Lulu, and Mara.

—Ptolemy Tompkins

Appendix

The Answers Lie Within Us All

The knower of the mystery of sound knows
the mystery of the whole universe.
—Hazrat Inayat Khan (1882–1927)

Who are we?
Where did we come from?
Where are we going?

I learned from my journey that a true seeker must go deep into his or her own consciousness to come closer to realizing the truth of our existence. Simply reading and hearing about other people's experiences and ideas is not enough. As we have seen, scientific and religious dogma is not always correct and it is important to develop a strong level of trust in our own internal guidance system rather than blindly following the so-called experts.

It is not necessary to experience an NDE or another type of external event to provide this knowledge—it can be intentionally cultivated. Long-term meditators and mystics have demonstrated this for millennia. It took me a few years after my coma to understand this, but I finally realized I had to develop a regular pattern of meditation to expand my relationship with the spiritual realm. I found that I could revisit some of the most profound supra-physical realms of my deep-coma journey through sound-enhanced meditations that were, for me, a form of centering prayer. Those meditations helped me not only to reaccess elements of my coma journey, but to reach levels deep within consciousness. Just as sound had facilitated the transitions in my coma journey to deeper and more expanded realms, sound can play a significant role for us all—here and now.

At the time I lapsed into coma in November 2008, I had been working for the Focused Ultrasound Surgery Foundation for more than a year. My main function there was to coordinate global medical research in this powerful and innovative technology, which I had first encountered while working on the Intraoperative Magnetic Resonance Imaging (iMRI) project at Harvard Medical School in the early 1990s. In that role, I was learning about the broad spectrum of beneficial interactions that sound could have with matter. Specifically, I was seeing how the thermal and mechanical effects of ultrasound—the sound of a frequency above 20,000 cycles per second, or hertz (Hz), the upper limit of human hearing—could be guided through advanced magnetic resonance imaging (or MRI) and revolutionize medicine through a range of therapies. It turns out that my work there was just scratching the surface of how sound can influence the material world.

As readers of *Proof of Heaven* know, music, sound, and vibration were key to accessing the full spectrum of spiritual realms during my NDE—from the Spinning Melody of pure white light that rescued me from the Earthworm's-Eye View, serving as a portal into the ultra-real Gateway Valley, to the angelic choirs whose chants and hymns prompted my ascendance beyond that idyllic heavenly valley through higher dimensions until I finally reached the Core, far beyond all space and time. It was in the Core that I felt the thunderous awe of *Om*, the sound that I associated with that infinitely powerful, knowing, and loving Being, that Deity beyond naming or description—God.

One of the most common questions after my presentations is whether I remember the music, especially the Spinning Melody. The answer is that I have lost the memory of those magical sounds. But I have worked with several people in an effort to recover them in this earthly realm. Saskia Moore, who lives in London, found some correlation between elements that I identified from the music of my NDE and similar music she has identified among other NDE-ers in her "Dead Symphony" project.*

One extraordinary experience with sound and medita-

---

*For more on Moore's "Dead Symphony" project, visit http://saskiamoore.tumblr.com /deadsymphony.

tion arose from a session I spent with Alexandre Tannous, an ethnomusicologist and sound researcher who has been studying and practicing sound therapy. I first met Alexandre at a Bioethics Forum conference in Madison, Wisconsin, on death and dying. He mesmerized the entire audience with his enchanting sound meditation, using gongs, chimes, and antique Tibetan singing bowls.

A few weeks later, I met him for a private session in his studio in New York City. He provided me with an astonishing sound journey that offered an experience completely out of this universe. I was shocked at the reality of the world I entered through the sounds he produced—a world with completely different laws of physics. I saw gently waving grasses beside a flowing river and witnessed the rotation of a nearby galaxy in the night skies. My experience of time was upended: it felt like a journey of many hours, but actually took only a fraction of that time. My description might suggest a psychedelic drug experience, but this extraordinary journey resulted from sound alone.

That's because *everything is a vibration.* Our sensory systems, especially the eyes and ears, process information through the frequencies of vibrating waves, whether of electromagnetic radiation (light visible to the human eye) or sound waves in air striking the eardrum. Likewise, the current neuroscientific model of brain function relies on information processing as being wholly the result of vibrations—of the temporal-spatial firing patterns of the enormously rich network of neurons in the human brain. Neuroscience would say everything you have ever experienced is nothing more than those electrochemical vibrations in the brain—a *model* of reality, not reality itself.

Before my coma, I knew little of the importance of sound in certain religious and meditative traditions. Since then, I have learned a great deal about the significance of the Om sound, in particular, especially within the Hindu tradition, where it is the primary sound used in the chanting of mantras. Om has been described as the primordial vibration that gave rise to the matter in our world today. My experience in the Core showed me that Om is indeed at the origin of all existence.

Much of my current research thus involves the use of sound (music, and other manipulations of the various frequencies of sound) to produce deep transcendental states of consciousness. Through this research, I have been trying to take my physical brain "out of the equation," to neutralize the information-processing of my neocortex—to set my awareness free. I sought to mimic the grand enhancement of conscious awareness that I had first experienced due to my meningitis (and the ensuing neocortical destruction) when I followed the clear white light (the Spinning Melody) from the Earthworm's-Eye View up into the brilliant ultra-reality of the Gateway Valley. The angelic choirs there provided another portal leading through higher dimensions to the Core. I surmised that I might use sound to revisit the realms of my deep coma odyssey, and that I might do so by synchronizing my brain waves with specific frequencies.

At its simplest, this involves the use of slightly different frequency tones presented through headphones to the two ears. For example, presenting a 100 Hz signal to one ear and a 104 Hz tone to the other yields the sensation of a 4 Hz wavering sound, a "binaural beat," of the difference between the two inputs. The "beat" sound does not exist as such outside the brain—it is not a "sound" that others would hear.

The neural circuit in the lower brain stem that generates the binaural beat is adjacent to a primitive circuit that, according to modern neuroscientific ideas about consciousness, is the fundamental timing mechanism for binding many separate neural modules into the "oneness" of conscious perception. My theory is that this allows the beat frequency to drive, or "entrain," the dominant electrical activity in the neocortex, and thus modulate its overall function.

It was in this context that I encountered Karen Newell in November 2011. Karen had a depth of knowledge, wisdom, and experience that complemented my own journey at many levels. She and audio composer/engineer Kevin Kossi, co-founders of Sacred Acoustics, had been working together for almost a year on using these types of synchronized frequencies to regularly attain altered states of awareness. I came to realize that their techniques might have tremendous potential in helping me reach those extraordinary spiritual realms I wanted to revisit. Upon first listening to their recordings, I was astonished at their power to liberate my awareness from the limitations of my brain. Part of their technique includes drawing from frequencies and harmonics found in the natural world. They are also inspired by the acoustics found in ancient sacred structures.

Appendix

Our ancient ancestors were aware of sound as a tool for accessing the spiritual realms. The Princeton Engineering Anomalies Research (PEAR) group, established in 1979, spent several decades studying the role of consciousness in physical reality, including investigations into archeoacoustics (the study of the acoustical properties of ancient ritual sites). One PEAR study* in Great Britain involved the measurement of acoustical resonance in ancient man-made structures. Despite the many different shapes and sizes of various enclosures, many were found to resonate at a similar frequency range of 95 to 120 Hz. This span is similar to that found in the human male vocal range. Some have speculated that human chanting took place in these locations, enhanced by the resonance, in order to access nonlocal states of awareness.

According to acoustics research performed in the Great Pyramid of Giza in Egypt, the builders deliberately included features that created resonance at the lower frequency ranges (1–8 Hz) associated with transcendental meditative and dream states. Modern visitors who spend time inside the King's Chamber within the Great Pyramid report mystical experiences when producing vocal chants and other sounds. Many of the magnificent medieval cathedrals around the world are also known for their acoustical qualities, which allow organ music and choral hymns to resonate with the building's structure and provide an uplifting spiritual experience to participants. This is especially evident at the Cathédrale Notre-Dame de Chartres in France. Like the Great Pyramid, Chartres was constructed

---

*http://www.princeton.edu/~pear/pdfs/1995-acoustical-resonances-ancient-structures.pdf.

to enhance specific harmonics. Gregorian chants are particularly powerful there. Their purpose was to help listeners and vocalists alike connect more personally to the Divine.

As a neurosurgeon, I had known for decades that only a minuscule fraction of the neocortex is actually devoted to generating and understanding speech and producing one's conscious thoughts. Beginning in the early 1980s, the experiments of Benjamin Libet and others revealed that the little voice in our head, the "linguistic brain," is not even the decision-maker of our consciousness. This linguistic brain, tightly linked with ego and notions of self, is only a spectator—it is informed of conscious decisions 100–150 milliseconds after such decisions are made. The origin of those choices is a far deeper mystery. Dr. Wilder Penfield, one of the most renowned neurosurgeons of the twentieth century, declared in his 1975 book *The Mystery of the Mind* that consciousness is not *created* by the physical brain. He knew from decades of work electrically stimulating the brains of awake patients that what we refer to as free will, consciousness, or mind seems to influence the physical brain from "outside," and is *not* created by it.

The true depth of accessible consciousness wasn't clear to me until after my coma, and that depth has become all the more evident since I began working with Sacred Acoustics. These sound-enhanced meditations have helped me turn off that little voice in my head, that constant flow of thoughts (which is *not* our consciousness), and connect to the inner *observer* of those thoughts, bringing my awareness closer to my own true being. By temporarily disabling the chatter of the linguistic brain (ego/self), so associated with fear and anxiety, and cultivating our awareness through meditation, we begin to access the true nature of consciousness, and of existence.

Like differing NDE reports, each individual will experience this awareness in different ways. Through my meditations, I have been quite successful at returning to those realms I first encountered deep in my coma. I have also been able to sense and communicate with my father's soul, so glaringly absent from my near-death experience. Others have reported improved focus, remarkable creative inspirations, the recovery of lost memories from childhood, expanded awareness, guidance, and intuition. Some have even connected directly with nonphysical realms and with the awe-inspiring Oneness of universal consciousness. Each of our journeys is unique—the possibilities are unlimited. The gift of awareness brings us the potential to explore for ourselves the true nature of consciousness and our personal connection to all that is.

As each of us awakens to the fact that our individual awareness is part of a much grander universal consciousness, humanity will enter the greatest phase in all of recorded history, in which we will gain a deeper understanding of the fundamental nature of all existence. This will involve the consolidation of wisdom over millennia, a coalescence of science and spirituality, and a convergence of the greatest concepts about the nature of our existence. The answers lie within us all.

Are you ready?

Bibliography

Alexander, Eben. *Proof of Heaven: A Neurosurgeon's Journey into the Afterlife*. New York: Simon & Schuster, 2012.

Alexander, Eben, and Karen Newell. *Seeking Heaven: Sound Journeys into the Beyond*. New York: Simon & Schuster Audiobooks, 2013.

Anderson, William. *Dante the Maker*. London: Hutchison, 1983

———. *The Face of Glory: Creativity, Consciousness and Civilization*. London: Trafalgar Square, 1996.

Arkle, William. *A Geography of Consciousness*. London: Neville Spearman, 1974.
Arkle is little known today, but an extraordinary thinker whose experiences overlap remarkably with mine.

Bache, Christopher. *Dark Night, Early Dawn: Steps to a Deep Ecology of Mind*. Albany: State University of New York Press, 2000.

Baker, Mark C., and Stewart Goetz, eds. *The Soul Hypothesis: Investigations into the Existence of the Soul*. London: Continuum International, 2011.

Blackhirst, Rodney. *Primordial Alchemy and Modern Religion: Essays on Traditional Cosmology*. San Rafael, CA: Sophia Perennis, 2008.
It is surprising how many widely differing views there are on what Plato really thought. This brilliant collection of essays is essential reading for anyone interested in what Plato means to us today.

Bucke, Maurice. *Cosmic Consciousness: A Study in the Evolution of the Human Mind*. New York: Dutton, 1956.

Chalmers, David J. *The Conscious Mind: In Search of a Fundamental Theory*. Oxford: Oxford University Press, 1996.

Corbin, Henry. *The Man of Light in Iranian Sufism*. Translated by Nancy Pearson. Boulder, CO: Omega Publications, 1994.

———. *Spiritual Body and Celestial Earth*. Translated by Nancy Pearson. Princeton: Princeton University Press, 1989.

———. *Alone with the Alone: Creative Imagination in the Sufism of Ibn 'Arabi*. Translated by Ralph Manheim. Princeton: Princeton University Press, 1998.

Crookall, Robert. *The Supreme Adventure: Analyses of Psychic Communications*. London: James Clarke, 1961

Dalai Lama (His Holiness the Dalai Lama). *A Profound Mind: Cultivating Wisdom in Everyday Life*. New York: Harmony Books, 2012.

———. *The Universe in a Single Atom: The Convergence of Science and Spirituality*. New York: Broadway Books, 2005.

De Chardin, Teilhard. *Christianity and Evolution: Reflections on Science and Religion*. Translated by René Hague. San Diego, CA: Harcourt Brace Jovanovich, 1971.

———. *The Heart of Matter*. Translated by René Hague. San Diego, CA: Harcourt Brace Jovanovich, 1978.

Delbrück, Max. *Mind from Matter: An Essay on Evolutionary Epistemology*. Palo Alto, CA: Blackwell Scientific Publications, 1986.

Devereux, Paul. *Stone Age Soundtracks: The Acoustic Archaeology of Ancient Sites*. London: Vega, 2002.

Dossey, Larry. *One Mind: How Our Individual Mind Is Part of a*

Greater Consciousness and Why It Matters. Carlsbad, CA: Hay House, 2013.
Dossey sums up the latest research into consciousness and its implications for all of us.

————. *The Power of Premonitions: How Knowing the Future Can Shape Our Lives.* New York: Dutton, 2009.

Elder, Paul. *Eyes of an Angel: Soul Travel, Spirit Guides, Soul Mates and the Reality of Love.* Charlottesville, VA: Hampton Roads, 2005.

Elkington, David, and Paul Howard Ellson. *In the Name of the Gods: The Mystery of Resonance and the Prehistoric Messiah.* Sherborne, UK: Green Man Press, 2001.

Findlay, J. N. *The Transcendence of the Cave.* London: George Allen & Unwin, 1967.

Fontana, David. *Is There an Afterlife? A Comprehensive Overview of the Evidence.* Ropley, UK: IFF Books, 2005.

————. *Life Beyond Death: What Should We Expect?* London: Watkins, 2009.
Fontana is one of my and Ptolemy's favorite authors. Both these books are classics.

Fox, Mark. *Religion, Spirituality and the Near-Death Experience.* New York: Routledge, 2002.

————. *Spiritual Encounters with Unusual Light Phenomena: Lightforms.* Cardiff: University of Wales Press, 2008.

Godwin, Joscelyn. *The Golden Thread: The Ageless Wisdom of the Western Mystery Traditions.* Wheaton, IL: Quest Books, 2007.

Groll, Ursula. *Swedenborg and New Paradigm Science.* Translated by Nicholas Goodrick-Clarke. West Chester, PA: Swedenborg Foundation Publishers, 2000.

Bibliography

Grosso, Michael. *The Final Choice: Playing the Survival Game*. Walpole, NH: Stillpoint, 1985.

Guggenheim, Bill, and Judy Guggenheim. *Hello from Heaven!* New York: Bantam Books, 1995.

Hale, Susan Elizabeth. *Sacred Space, Sacred Sound: The Acoustic Mysteries of Holy Places*. Wheaton, IL: Quest Books, 2007.

Happold, F. C. *Mysticism: A Study and an Anthology*. 3rd ed. New York: Penguin, 1990.
A fantastic survey of mystical experiences of all kinds, and one of Ptolemy's favorites.

Hardy, Alister. *The Spiritual Nature of Man*. New York: Clarendon Press, 1979.

Head, Joseph and Cranston, S. L. *Reincarnation: The Phoenix Fire Mystery: An East-West Dialogue on Death and Rebirth from the Worlds of Religion, Science, Psychology, Philosophy, Art, and Literature, and from Great Thinkers of the Past and Present*. New York: Julian Press, 1977.

Hogan, R. Craig. *Your Eternal Self*. Normal, IL: Greater Reality Publications, 2008.

Holden, Janice Miner, Bruce Greyson, and Debbie James, eds. *The Handbook of Near-Death Experiences: Thirty Years of Investigation*. Santa Barbara, CA: Praeger, 2009.

Houshmand, Zara, Robert B. Livingston, and B. Alan Wallace., eds. *Consciousness at the Crossroads: Conversations with the Dalai Lama on Brain Science and Buddhism*. Ithaca, NY: Snow Lion, 1999.

Jahn, Robert G., and Brenda J. Dunne. *Margins of Reality: The Role of Consciousness in the Physical World*. New York: Harcourt Brace Jovanovich, 1987.

Bibliography

Jung, C. G. *Memories, Dreams, Reflections.* Recorded and edited by Aniela Jaffé. New York: Vintage, 1987.

———. *Synchronicity: An Acausal Connecting Principle.* Princeton: Princeton University Press, 2010.

Kason, Yvonne, and Teri Degler. *A Farther Shore: How Near-Death and Other Extraordinary Experiences Can Change Ordinary Lives.* New York: HarperCollins, 1994. (Republished as *Farther Shores*, iUniverse, 2008.)

Kelly, Edward F., Emily Williams Kelly, Adam Crabtree, Alan Gauld, Michael Grosso, and Bruce Greyson. *Irreducible Mind: Toward a Psychology for the 21st Century.* Lanham, MD: Rowman & Littlefield, 2007.

Knight, F. Jackson. *Elysion: On Ancient Greek and Roman Ideas Concerning a Life After Death.* London: Rider, 1970.
A truly revolutionary look by a great scholar at what the ancients really thought about death and the afterlife.

Kübler-Ross, Elisabeth. *On Life After Death.* Berkeley, CA: Ten Speed Press, 1991.

Lachman, Gary. *The Caretakers of the Cosmos: Living Responsibly in an Unfinished World.* London: Floris Books, 2013.
How do we fit the discoveries being made about the spiritual world into how to live on the earth here and now? Lachman gives a fascinating survey of the possible answers.

LeShan, Lawrence. *A New Science of the Paranormal: The Promise of Psychical Research.* Wheaton, IL: Quest Books, 2009.

Libet, B., C. A. Gleason, E. W. Wright, and D. K. Pearl. "Time of conscious intention to act in relation to onset of cerebral activity (readiness-potential): The unconscious initiation of a freely voluntary act." *Brain* 106 (1983): 623–42.

Bibliography

Libet, Benjamin. *Mind Time: The Temporal Factor in Consciousness.* Cambridge, MA: Harvard University Press, 2004.

Lockwood, Michael. *Mind, Brain & the Quantum: The Compound 'I.'* Oxford: Basil Blackwell, 1989.

Lorimer, David. *Survival? Body, Mind and Death in the Light of Psychic Experience.* London: Routledge & Kegan Paul, 1984.

———. *Whole in One: The Near-Death Experience and the Ethic of Interconnectedness.* New York: Arkana, 1991.

MacGreggor, Geddes: *Reincarnation as a Christian Hope.* London: Macmillan, 1982.

McMoneagle, Joseph. *Mind Trek: Exploring Consciousness, Time, and Space Through Remote Viewing.* Charlottesville, VA: Hampton Roads, 1993.

Maxwell, Meg and Tschudin, Verena. *Seeing the Invisible: Modern Religious and Other Transcendent Experiences.* London: Arkana, 1990.
An excellent investigation of contemporary mystical/transcendent experiences with a large sampling of narratives from Alister Hardy's Religious Experience Research Center.

Mayer, Elizabeth Lloyd. *Extraordinary Knowing: Science, Skepticism, and the Inexplicable Powers of the Human Mind.* New York: Bantam, 2007.

———. *Remote Viewing Secrets: A Handbook.* Charlottesville, VA: Hampton Roads, 2000.

Medhananda. *With Medhananda on the Shores of Infinity.* Pondicherry, India: Sri Mira Trust, 1998.

Monroe, Robert A. *Far Journeys.* New York: Doubleday, 1985.

———. *Journeys Out of the Body.* New York: Doubleday, 1971.

Bibliography

————. *Ultimate Journey.* New York: Doubleday, 1994.

Moody, Raymond A., Jr. *Life After Life: The Investigation of a Phenomenon—Survival of Bodily Death.* New York: Harper-Collins, 2001.

Moody, Raymond, Jr., and Paul Perry. *Glimpses of Eternity: Sharing a Loved One's Passage from This Life to the Next.* New York: Guideposts, 2010.

Moorjani, Anita. *Dying to Be Me: My Journey from Cancer, to Near Death, to True Healing.* Carlsbad, CA: Hay House, 2012.

Murphy, Michael. *The Future of the Body: Explorations into the Further Evolution of Human Nature.* New York: Tarcher, 1993.
Murphy's book is unsurpassed as a catalog of human possibilities, and is a treasure trove of information.

Nicolaus, Georg. *C. G. Jung and Nikolai Berdyaev: Individuation and the Person.* New York: Routledge, 2011.
A brilliant book on Jung and another great visionary mind of the twentieth century.

Pagels, Elaine. *Beyond Belief: The Secret Gospel of Thomas.* New York: Random House, 2003

————. *The Gnostic Gospels.* New York: Vintage Books, 1979.

Penfield, Wilder. *The Mystery of the Mind: A Critical Study of Consciousness and the Human Brain.* Princeton: Princeton University Press, 1975.

Penrose, Roger. *Cycles of Time: An Extraordinary New View of the Universe.* New York: Knopf, 2010.

————. *The Emperor's New Mind.* Oxford: Oxford University Press, 1989.

————. *The Road to Reality: A Complete Guide to the Laws of the Universe.* New York: Vintage Books, 2007.

———. *Shadows of the Mind.* Oxford: Oxford University Press, 1994.

Penrose, Roger, Malcolm Longair, Abner Shimony, Nancy Cartwright, and Stephen Hawking. *The Large, the Small, and the Human Mind.* Cambridge: Cambridge University Press, 1997.

Puryear, Herbert Bruce. *Why Jesus Taught Reincarnation: A Better News Gospel.* Scottsdale, AZ: New Paradigm Press, 1992.

Radin, Dean. *The Conscious Universe: The Scientific Truth of Psychic Phenomena.* New York: HarperCollins, 1997.

———. *Entangled Minds: Extrasensory Experiences in a Quantum Reality.* New York: Simon & Schuster, 2006.

———. *Supernormal: Science, Yoga, and the Evidence for Extraordinary Psychic Abilities.* New York: Random House, 2013.

Raine, Kathleen. *W. B. Yeats and the Learning of the Imagination.* Dallas: Dallas Institute Publications, 1999.

Ramakrishna, Sri. *The Gospel of Sri Ramakrishna.* Translated by Swami Nikhilananda. New York: Ramakrishna-Vivekananda Center, 1980.

Ring, Kenneth, and Sharon Cooper. *Mindsight: Near-Death and Out-of-Body Experiences in the Blind.* Palo Alto, CA: William James Center for Consciousness Studies at the Institute of Transpersonal Psychology, 1999.

Ring, Kenneth, and Evelyn Elsaesser Valarino. *Lessons from the Light: What We Can Learn from the Near-Death Experience.* New York: Insight Books, 1998.

Robinson, Edward. *The Original Vision: A Study of the Religious Experience of Childhood.* New York: Seabury Press, 1983.
A beautiful exploration of the spiritual experiences of children, using much of the Hardy material discussed in this book.

Bibliography

Rosenblum, Bruce, and Fred Kuttner. *Quantum Enigma: Physics Encounters Consciousness.* New York: Oxford University Press, 2006.

Russell, Peter. *From Science to God: A Physicist's Journey into the Mystery of Consciousness.* San Francisco: New World Library, 2004.

Schrödinger, Erwin. *What Is Life? With Mind and Matter and Autobiographical Sketches* (Canto Classics). Cambridge: Cambridge University Press, 1992.

Schwartz, Stephan A. *Opening to the Infinite: The Art and Science of Nonlocal Awareness.* Buda, TX: Nemoseen Media, 2007.

Sheldrake, Rupert. *Science Set Free: 10 Paths to New Discovery.* New York: Deepak Chopra Books, 2012.

Singer, Thomas, *The Vision Thing: Myth, Politics and Psyche in the New World.* New York: Routledge, 2000.

Smith, Huston. *The Way Things Are: Conversations with Huston Smith on the Spiritual Life.* Edited by Phil Cousineau. Los Angeles: University of California Press, 2003.

Smoley, Richard. *The Dice Game of Shiva: How Consciousness Creates the Universe.* San Francisco: New World Library, 2009.

———. *Hidden Wisdom: A Guide to the Western Inner Traditions* (with Jay Kinney). Wheaton, IL: Quest Books, 2006.

———. *Inner Christianity: A Guide to the Esoteric Tradition.* Boston: Shambhala, 2002.
Smoley is a crucial guide to the ancient traditions, and to how a greater understanding of those traditions can make our lives today more meaningful.

Stevenson, Ian. *Children Who Remember Previous Lives: A Question of Reincarnation.* Rev. ed. Jefferson, NC: McFarland, 2001.

Sudman, Natalie. *Application of Impossible Things: A Near Death Experience.* Huntsville, AR: Ozark Mountain, 2012.
One of the most astounding and significant near-death experiences ever recounted.

Sussman, Janet Iris. *The Reality of Time.* Fairfield, IA: Time Portal, 2005.

———. *Timeshift: The Experience of Dimensional Change.* Fairfield, IA: Time Portal, 1996.

Talbot, Michael. *The Holographic Universe.* New York: Harper-Collins, 1991.

Tarnas, Richard. *Cosmos and Psyche: Intimations of a New World View.* New York: Plume, 2007.

———. *The Passion of the Western Mind: Understanding the Ideas That Have Shaped Our World View.* New York: Ballantine Books, 1993.

Tart, Charles T. *The End of Materialism: How Evidence of the Paranormal Is Bringing Science and Spirit Together.* Oakland, CA: New Harbinger, 2009.

Taylor, Jill Bolte. *My Stroke of Insight: A Brain Scientist's Personal Journey.* New York: Penguin, 2006.

TenDam, Hans. *Exploring Reincarnation.* Translated by A. E. J. Wils. London: Arkana, 1990.

Tompkins, Ptolemy. *The Modern Book of the Dead: A Revolutionary Perspective on Death, the Soul, and What Really Happens in the Life to Come.* New York: Atria Books, 2012.

Traherne, Thomas. *Selected Poems and Prose.* New York: Penguin Classics, 1992.

Tucker, J. B. *Life Before Life: A Scientific Investigation of Children's Memories of Previous Lives.* New York: St. Martin's Press, 2005.

Bibliography

Uždavinys, Algis. *The Golden Chain: An Anthology of Pythagorean and Platonic Philosophy.* Bloomington, IN: World Wisdom Books, 2004.

Van Dusen, Wilson. *The Presence of Other Worlds: The Psychological and Spiritual Findings of Emanuel Swedenborg.* New York: Chrysalis Books, 2004.
An extremely readable book about Swedenborg's often dense and difficult writing and the implications of his life and work.

Van Lommel, Pim. *Consciousness Beyond Life: The Science of Near-Death Experience.* New York: HarperCollins, 2010.
Another modern classic.

Von Franz, Marie-Louise. *On Death & Dreams.* Boston: Shambhala, 1987.

———. *Psyche and Matter.* Boston: Shambhala, 2001.

Walker, Benjamin. *Beyond the Body: The Human Double and the Astral Planes.* London: Routledge & Kegan Paul, 1974.

Weiss, Brian L. *Many Lives, Many Masters.* New York: Fireside, 1988.

Whiteman J. H. M. *The Mystical Life: An Outline of Its Nature and Teachings from the Evidence of Direct Experience.* London: Faber & Faber, 1961.

———. *Old & New Evidence on the Meaning of Life: The Mystical World-View and Inner Contest.* London: Colin Smythe, 1968.

Wigner, Eugene. "The Unreasonable Effectiveness of Mathematics in the Natural Sciences." *Communications in Pure and Applied Mathematics* 13, no. 1 (1960).

Wilber, Ken., ed. *Quantum Questions.* Boston: Shambhala, 1984.

Wilson, Colin. *Afterlife: An Investigation.* New York: Doubleday, 1987.

Bibliography

Yeats, William Butler. *The Collected Works of W. B. Yeats, Volume III: Autobiographies*. New York: Touchstone, 1999.

Zukav, Gary. *The Dancing Wu Li Masters*. New York: William Morrow and Company, Inc., 1979.

———. *Seat of the Soul*. New York: Fireside Press, 1989.

Index

Index

caduceus, 37, 89
Campbell, Joseph, 25, 27, 128
carbon, xii–xiii, xvi, 88–89
Cave and the Light, The (Herman), 17
cerebellum, 54
chanting, 139–41, 143–44
chemistry, xiii, xv
children/childhood, 71, 81–83, 85, 87,
    100, 102, 105, 113–14, 118, 121,
    145
Christianity, xiv, xxxiv, 2, 6, 9, 28, 55,
    88, 101, 117, 130
circles, symbolism of, 131
coincidence, 30, 40
    See also synchronicity
Coleridge, Samuel Taylor, 1
connection, xvii, xxxiii, 2, 79, 81, 86–88,
    93, 119–21, 131, 144–45
consciousness, xxi–xxv, xxvii, 2, 17–18,
    23, 43, 47, 54, 56
Corbin, Henry, 57*n*, 130
Core, xxviii–xxix, 26, 139, 141
Crosby, Stills and Nash, 40
crypts, 26

dancing, 116–17
Dante, 111
Dark Night, Early Dawn (Bache), 118
"Dead Symphony" project, 139
Demeter, 7
demons, 55
depth, explained, ix–x
Descartes, René, 42–43, 48
destiny, 26, 65, 125, 128, 131
devils, 115
Divine Comedy (Dante), 111
divinity, xxviii–xxix, 25, 57–58, 121–22,
    144
Division of Perceptual Studies
    (DOPS), 84–85
dogmatic religion, 9, 49, 51, 64, 68, 70,
    137
"dogmatic science," xxv, xxvii, 64
Dogon people, 30
dreams, xxxi, 25–26, 38, 55, 82, 86, 143

Dreamtime, 117
drugs, 80–81, 140
Duke University Medical Center, 46
Durkheim, Emile, 61–62

Earthworm's-Eye View, xxvii, 11, 139,
    141
Ebert, Roger, 125–28
Eccles, John C., xxiii
Egypt, xiv, 31, 143
Einstein, Albert, 58
electrochemical activity, ix, xi, 84, 141
electrons, xiii, xvi, 103
elements, xii–xiii, xv–xvi, 89, 91, 105
Eleusinian mysteries, 7
Emerald Tablet, 105
Emerson, Ralph Waldo, 61
emotions, xi, xvii, 8, 91, 99
Empyrean, 111
Entlich, Don, 37–40
Er (soldier), 3
Erasmus, Desiderius, 107
eternal life, 8
evidence, 18, 26, 63–64, 67, 83, 118
existence:
    afterlife and, 48, 100, 118
    ancients and, 10, 13
    memory and, 3
    physical, 16
    Plato and, 16
    reality and, 103–5
    spiritual and, 104–5, 111, 141, 145
    time and, 82
    truth and, 61, 137
existentialism, 16
external, 56, 138
Extraordinary Knowing (Mayer), 34

faith, 62–63, 88, 98, 115
familiarity, xix, 92, 112, 120
Farther Shores (Kason), 22
fear:
    consciousness and, 145
    death and, 10–12
    spirituality and, xxix

160

Index

Fechner, Gustav, 52–54, 62, 99
Fertile Crescent, 7
Flatland (Abbott), 98
flowers, 47, 78, 110–13, 116–17, 119, 125
Focused Ultrasound Surgery Foundation, 138
folklore, 48
foxes, 48–50
friendship, xvii
funerals, 3, 32, 111
   See also burial

Galileo, 48
Gateway, xxix, 26, 139, 141
Ghazali, al-, xii
ghosts, 10
Gifts of Heaven, xxxiii, 13
Goethe, Johann Wolfgang von, 51, 54, 62, 99
gold, xv–xvii
golden scarab, 31
golden thread, xxxiii, 88, 119
goodness, xvii, 58, 97
Goswami, Amit, xxiv
Great Pyramid of Giza, 143
Greece (ancient), ix, 2, 4, 7, 10, 12, 28, 128
greeters, 113
Gregorian chants, 144
Greyson, Bruce, 84, 135
Groll, Ursula, 56
growth, 113–15
Gulf Stream, 67

Hades (god), 7
hallucination, xxxi, 82, 126
happiness, 9, 19, 78, 97, 99, 101, 120
Hardy, Alister, xxxiv*n*, 62*n*, 67–71, 77–79, 81–83, 85–86, 97, 120*n*, 130
Harvard Medical School, 138
heaven:
   ancients and, 6–7
   childhood and, 82

Christianity and, 6
dancing and, 116–17
initiation and, 28
knowledge of, 85, 87
material world and, 48, 130–32
mysticism and, 57–58
NDEs and, 33–34, 78, 92, 112
Plato and, 2, 4
science and, 62, 64–65
sky and, 125
spiritual and, 9–11, 48, 52–53, 55–57, 89, 100, 122, 130–32
study of, 17–18
symbolism and, 111, 116
heirs, 88–89
Heisenberg, Werner, xxii, xxiv
hell, xxviii, 55, 115, 131
Heraclitus, x
heresy, xv
Hering, Jean, xxx
Herman, Arthur, 17
Hero with a Thousand Faces, The (Campbell), 25
heroes, 25–27, 60–61, 128
Hinduism, 60, 91, 118, 141
Homer, 10–11, 15
Homeric Hymns, 11*n*
human potential movement, 69
Huxley, Aldous, 83, 127–28

Ibn 'Arabi, 57
Iliad (Homer), 10
illusion, x, 30, 47, 110, 113, 126–28
immortality, xiii, xv
Inanna (goddess), 7–8
individuality, 104, 118
initiation:
   afterlife and, 11
   heroic journey and, 26–28
   identity and, 11–12, 51
   Plato and, 5, 15, 89
   rebirth and, 8–9
   religion and, 5–9
   science and, 18–19, 37

Index

Index

Index

Index